UNDERSTANDING CHRISTIAN DRUG AND ALCOHOL RECOVERY.©

Ronald Simmons

Published and Distributed by:
Free N One Books
PO Box 561592
Los Angeles, California 90056
(323) 855-4695

First Printing, There is a Ram in the Bush
August 1988

Second Printing, Understanding Christian
Drug and Alcohol Recovery
January 2001

Third Printing Understanding Christian
Drug and Alcohol Recovery January 2005

Fourth Printing Understanding Christian
Drug and Alcohol Recovery October 2011

Fifth Printing Understanding Christian
Drug and Alcohol Recovery June 2014

ISBN: 978-1475027938

About The Author

Born and raised in Los Angeles, Ron celebrates over 23 years of being free from drugs and alcohol. Ron is married to Yolonda Simmons and they have three children; twins Daniel and Danyell, 24 years of age; and Quianna who is 21. Their children are currently attending San Diego State University, in San Diego, California

Ron attended El Camino College and later attended UCLA. There he received a certificate in Drug and Alcohol Counseling. He has received numerous awards and commendations from the Mayor of Los Angeles, the Senate, and various other acknowledgements for his work in the field of recovery.

Ron lectures nationally on Drug and Alcohol Recovery. Ron co-founded the nationally run organization Free N One (Free from Drugs & Alcohol and One in Christ). Free N One assists Churches in establishing successful out-patient Drug and Alcohol Recovery programs in their Church.

For 18 years Elder Ron Simmons was Executive Director of Transition House, a Christ-centered drug and alcohol in-house program owned by the First Jurisdiction of Southern California of the Church of God in Christ, where Bishop Charles E. Blake is the Prelate. The success of this program is already being highly recognized by the recovery community as an excellent model for Christian recovery homes.

After years of success with the Free N One outpatient program and as the director of Transition House, there have been many requests for written help in the form of an instructional manual. Mr. Simmons presented his first book <u>There Is A Ram In The Bush</u> in 1998. <u>Understanding Christian Drug & Alcohol Recovery</u> was released in January 2001 and two other projects are soon to be released.

Ronald Simmons was ordained as an Elder in the Church of God in Christ on June 11, 1999. Ron's sobriety date is April 22, 1981.

This book is dedicated to all facilitators, ministers, pastors, and front line soldiers that stand before God's people compelling them surrender to a better life!

I also dedicate this book to those who struggled to find freedom! Freedom is near. Look to Jesus the author and finisher of your faith!

Table of Contents

God
Grant Me The Serenity To Accept The Things I Can Not Change

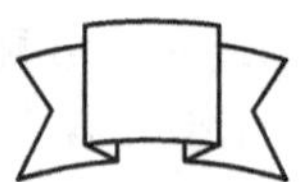

The Courage To Change The Things I Can

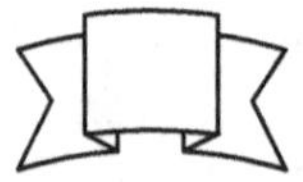

And The Wisdom To Know The Difference

Foreword

Substance abuse has been recognized by the medical community as a clinically verified disorder. Because alcoholism and drug addiction are considered "diseases" by most medical associations, much of the discussion concerning treatment has focused on the physiological and/or psycho-social factors that influence addiction and abusive behavior.

Ron Simmons has written this book to expose the root of the problem of addiction. He systematically examines the reasons and patterns that shape substance abusing. Ron's approach is built on the foundation that self-abuse -and abuse of others- is first a spiritual matter, with detrimental biological and environmental consequences.

Deliverance from substance abuse is possible and available through faith and obedience to the Word of God. This book speaks to the user and their loved ones, as well as enablers, ministers, educators, and medical/clinical professionals. Ron shares useful information that all of us can appreciate.

As a mental health professional and recovered substance abuser, Ron is more than qualified to speak on the subject, and through his personal journey, he has assisted in reclaiming many lives for Christ. He is currently the director of Transition House, a facility for recovering substance abusers. The center is owned and operated by the First Jurisdiction of Southern California of the Church of God in Christ, and under Ron's leadership, hundreds of men have successfully completed the program. Ron's commitment to the ministry of counseling and intervention in this area is a testament to the saving power of Jesus Christ. The Transition House provides a Christian-based recovery program that works because God's word is true, effective, and life changing.

Ron is also co-founder and CEO of Free N One. Free N One is an out-patient, Christ-centered drug and alcohol recovery program that is moving across this great nation and, because of that, it is changing the lives of thousands of people.

I hope that this book will inspire you, and in turn, may that inspiration motivate you toward a closer walk with God!

Charles E. Blake, Bishop
Presiding Bishop of the Church Of God In Christ

"The two most important days in your life is the day you are born….and the day you find out why"

~ Mark Twain

Preface

Should Christian residential recovery programs be more successful than conventional methods of recovery? Should the success rate in Christian outpatient programs be higher than secular run programs? This book was not written to disparage, nor challenge, traditional recovery programs; the ultimate goal is to bring to the forefront what we believe as Christians and our attempts to strive towards perfection.

As servants of God, the result of what we do should be nothing less than excellent. As Christians, our job is to reach for perfection, never being in competition with people or any organization. Our job as Christian facilitators, counselors, therapists, and psychologists, is to serve God's people to the best of our ability, while serving a perfect God. The Word of God has set high standards for us to follow; yet we must always recognize that even if we fail there is no failure in God.

Once we understand this truth, the question then becomes: "Can Christian recovery be perfected?" Through God's Word, that answer is a resounding: "Yes!" As Christians, we believe *we can do all things through Christ that strengthens us* as long as we *keep pressing towards the mark of the high calling in Christ Jesus.*

Christians have to say, "Yes, we can be the best we can be." Christians that work in this field of ministry must believe "yes" or walk away from this type of ministry.

Recovery is nothing new to God. It is found all through the Word of God and clearly explained in *Romans 12:2: "And do not be conformed to this world, but be transformed by the renewing of your mind, so that you may prove what the will of God is, that which is good and acceptable and perfect."* Transforming your mind is the key to sustained addiction recovery and living free, and we recognize this does not happen overnight. How to get from point A (addict/alcoholic) to point B (living free) is what we will attempt to share with you in this book.

Most addicts and alcoholics walk through the doors of the Church understanding something has to change. The challenge is what specifically needs to changed and how does the change take place. Psychologists today tell us that the disease of addiction centers in our mind, so it would be wise to start our battle with the mind.

One day a participant of Free N One, who was in the very early stages of his recovery, walked into my office and he was very frustrated. He was having a problem with all the changes that were taking place in his life. He cried out, "I think you guys are trying to brain wash me." My first response was laughter, but then I thought about what he said and realized that there was some truth in it. Anyone that gets paid on Friday, gives all his money to the dope man, and is broke on Saturday morning needs their brain washed. Anyone who drinks so much he can't remember how he got home or what he did the night before needs their brain washed. Anyone who has a hard time looking at himself or herself in the mirror because of the demoralizing and dangers things they did, needs their brain washed.

Understanding Christian Drug & Alcohol Recovery attempts to define this process in such a way that anyone who is called to this ministry will be able to lead any suffering addict/alcoholic on the road to recovery. The practicing addict/alcoholic who reads this book will understand the work that it takes to be free and also realize that the process does not happen overnight. The family member will finally see that there is nothing they can do to keep the addict/alcoholic from using and drinking. They will also realize the work that it takes for that loved one to be free.

The process of recovery is a systematic series of actions that leads the recovering person out of bondage, and into a safe place in Christ Jesus. Along with the 12 Spiritual Steps, the process helps in renewing the mind to create a positive change in the addictive person's thinking and actions. These steps are designed to take a recovering person by the hand and guide him/her to a better lifestyle in Christ Jesus. The steps single out character defects and replace them with moral standards. The recovering person slowly becomes what God wants him/her to be. In this case, the Word of God, and the 12 Spiritual Steps, assists the addict/alcoholic to lead a better life.

The disease of addiction is cunning, baffling and powerful. Some addicts/alcoholics can't stay free in an outpatient setting, but have to enter into a Christ-centered recovery home. In these homes, developing a personal relationship with our Lord and Savior Jesus Christ is the beginning of recovery. Learning how to get honest with others, and more importantly, with themselves, will be the next tool used in this ongoing process called recovery. Finally, facing their character defects along with uncovering years of hidden pain will be the hurdle that they all will have to address. In these recovery homes, they are also given tools that can help them to live a bondage-free lifestyle. I believe God called me to write this book to help educate the Church, and anyone who wants to be free.

Chapter *I*

Winning the War on Drug and Alcohol Addiction

Have you ever been bold enough to ask God, "What's really going on and why are we losing this war on drug and alcohol addiction?" Can you be honest enough with yourself, or with God, and admit we are losing this war against drug and alcohol addiction? A war we should be winning, simply because we serve the King of Kings, Jesus Christ our Lord.

All through the Bible, God has defeated Satan in many areas. Today we find ourselves losing battle after battle that we should be winning. All over the world, God's people are becoming hooked on some form of drug, or they are trying drugs or alcohol for the first time, and quickly becoming addicted.

Perfectly stable families are being destroyed because someone in that family has tried an legal or illegal drug for the first time and become a slave to it. If you don't know Jesus, it looks like Satan's plan is working perfectly.

This disease of addiction has presented itself boldly on the front steps of the Church and like Goliath it dares anyone to challenge its power. From the usher board to the choir stand, from the volunteers to the pulpit, men and women in the Church are falling victim to this disease called addiction. Whether it's directly, someone hooked on drugs or alcohol; or indirectly, a family member. The pain is just as great watching a loved one who is bound by this disease called addiction. In my years of working in the Christian Drug and Alcohol Recovery ministry, I have spoken with hundreds of ministers who have personally been affected by this demon.

As I talk to some of these individuals, I empathize with the pain they feel when someone close to them (whether family member, someone on their staff, or someone in their congregation) falls to this monster called "addiction." Some ministers lose hope, and even question their calling, because their many attempts to help addicts or alcoholics have failed. The pain is unbearable as they watch God's people return to drinking and using after they have given their best efforts to help them. After many failed attempts, some ministers avoid the problem altogether and send the practicing addict/alcoholic to a secular program. For many the pain of failure goes against the very faith they believe in and another failure is too much to deal with. However, most hold on tightly and believe God will make a way, one day. We believe that day is today!

Don't get me wrong, the Church has won, and is winning, many battles daily, and each battle won is still a great miracle, especially to the addict or alcoholic who is delivered and to his family and loved ones. Each time an addict or alcoholic surrenders and turns his or her life over to God; this miracle is equal to that of the parting the Red Sea, or raising

Lazarus from the dead. As a matter of fact, the dead have risen, and God's people rejoice as the addict or alcoholic surrenders and are set free.

We have seen it countless times; a practicing addict/alcoholic will come to the Lord and totally surrender their life. The spirit of God moves through this person and, as a result, this person is delivered with just a touch. Many have this testimony. We are blessed to witness these battles, but we are still losing the war, because many addicts/alcoholics continue to drink and use.

Those who have been delivered through the process of Christian recovery, and believe in Jesus with all our hearts and souls, find hope in a plan that can reach anyone who wants to be free. We, who are a part of this Free N One ministry, know this is a "winnable" war. We are a living testimony, declaring war on one of Satan's main strong holds - drug and alcohol addiction. In the days of our bondage, most of us walked through the doors of many Churches looking for help. We were hoping to be set free at a revival or healing service, or one touch from the man or woman of God, only to return to the walking dungeon of death called addiction. We tried not to drink or use but we just couldn't make it. We were hoping that something, or someone, would come and relieve us of the pain that had consumed our whole being.

So, the question has to be asked, "What is the Church doing wrong?" We know God's Word never fails, so that's not the problem. We are the children of God, who have been called to be a light for those who are still in darkness, so, "What are we doing wrong?" We have seen God move mountains in our lives and work miracles in countless others. We know that there is no failure in God, so we must seek the right answer. We must first understand that the most important question is not what we're doing wrong. We must also ask ourselves, "What can we do right to help people who are slowly dying from Satan's vicious attacks?"

We must first understand the enemy and how he attacks. Most people will be surprised to see that the enemy attacks long before the first drink or the first hit, in the form of disobedience, but Satan's job is to magnify the drug and alcohol usage. Even though we gather our armies and build up our warriors, they are not effective if we send them in the wrong direction. Today, the Church needs to come together as one to attack the enemy wherever he is for success in helping our people.

Next, you have to put the right people in the right place. Not everyone will be able to lead the charge into battle. For instance, not everybody can work in the children's church and not everybody can sing in the choir; so, surely, not everyone can work in the drug and alcohol ministry. Even though they may have a burden for God's people in this area, not everyone can do the work and be effective.

Have you ever listened to a bad choir sing? We praise God for their effort and give them credit for making a joyful noise unto the Lord, even though some of the notes they're singing haven't been invented yet. The same thing happens in the ministry of drug/alcohol addiction. If you put the wrong person in charge of this ministry, addicts and alcoholics will continue to use. We praise God for the effort, but the addict/alcoholic is still using. If you believe working with addicts and alcoholic is your ministry but no one finds freedom then something's wrong. Unlike hearing a few bad notes from a not-so-polished choir, we have lost a soul who could be free from this bondage if the right people are in place. We believe that the people whom God has delivered from the bondage of addiction or alcoholism should play a vital part in ministry. I would not want the First Lady of my church walking into some of the dope houses, gambling shacks, and gang-infested areas that I used to feel comfortable in. I believe this is my job, and the job of every person who has ever been delivered from that lifestyle.

People delivered from this type of lifestyle understand the mentality of those who are still consumed and trapped by it. People delivered from their addiction have mastered some of the games that are played in this arena. And many are sitting in congregation all over this city, all over this nation, all over this world. They are waiting to receive their marching orders to engage in battle. I am not saying that you have to be a recovering addict/alcoholic to fight on this battle field, no not at all. God can use who he wants to use. But in my years of working in this field those that have been delivered bring a special passion and dedication to the fight.

"Can't nobody tell the story like someone that been through it" This is why testimony is so important! *Revelation 12:11 And they have conquered him by the blood of the Lamb and by the word of their testimony, for they loved not their lives even unto death.* Today I am reminded that while living in that lifestyle God kept me safe and allowed me to go through everything that I went through, that I might go back to that type of hell and guide others out.

After these potential soldiers have been located they are educated and trained on how to apply the process of recovery. It is crucial they are equipped with the correct weapons to fight this battle and knowing when and how to use them. The Bible says, *"My people perish because of a lack of knowledge."* I have personally witnessed many Christ-centered drug and alcohol programs that looked great on paper, but were ineffective because they were using the wrong weapons for this particular battle.

Total abstinence is our goal from all mind altering substances. Learning how to live free from all Satan's devices that would lead a person back to the bondage they once were in. It is especially devastating when we watch a person celebrate 6 months, 9 months, 1 year clean and sober - giving God all the glory; then one day they turn around, and return to drinking and using. It is like pulling the plug in a sink filled with water, and watching the water go down the drain. The Bible says *it's like a dog returning to its own vomit.* It drains the hope out of the addict and everyone involved. Those seeking help need to know there is specific "spiritual medicine" in the Word of God that will keep them free from this addiction "one day at a time" *forever!* Knowing what medicine to administer will be the key.

I believe this book addresses these issues and many more. It is also an attempt to bring the Church together as one united front, standing together. One church standing alone has a slim chance, but many churches fighting together, as one will win more battles and on a larger scale.

In 1981, I was introduced to this process called recovery. It took me a whole year to get serious about working and living what I was learning. For the first year, I was excited about being free from the pains of everyday using. Participating in 12-step meetings, I learned enough to know that just being free from drugs and alcohol was not enough. It was at this time that I accepted Christ into my life, and my whole life turned around. As far as this new life was concerned, I was a babe in Christ and I was a babe at living. I didn't know how to pay bills, wash my own clothes, or cook for myself. I didn't know how to deal with my anger, or recognize my feelings when they showed up like a flood. Church was foreign to me. I didn't know the difference between a deacon and a minister, or a

Pastor and a Reverend, and Lord knows I did not have a clue as to what a Bishop's job was. Then you had denominations, even though we served the same God we disagree on how to serve Him, how to reach Him, and stay with Him; so, I avoided these subjects all together.

There were a few things that were certain; there was a God and I was not Him, and this God had all power. He delivered me from the pits of hell, and I was going to serve Him for the rest of my life.

Once I started living what I was learning in the rooms of recovery and what I was learning in the church, it was suggested that I get a sponsor. A sponsor is a person who has been through the process of recovery and is willing to help others walk through the process. (*See chapter II on "Why a Sponsor"*) Shortly after, I met a sponsor in the program who walk with me through the process of recovery, and a mentor in the Church who took me under his wings and walked with me according to the Word of God. I was slowly falling in love with this new life. In recovery, I found that I had a special love for all recovering people who were, after all, just like me. I understood those who were struggling to stay free from this disease called addiction. We went to 12-step meetings and sober functions together. People in the program became my new friends.

In the Church, I enjoyed praising God together with the saints. I also enjoyed going to Bible studies with other believers and learning how to be a Christian. As I grew in the Lord, I knew it was only God that kept me free from returning to my addictions. During this time, it was okay for me to be a babe in Christ, and a babe in recovery. I could ask all kinds of questions about recovery and about life, and not be embarrassed. It was explained to me that the only dumb question was an unasked question.

As my relationship with God grew, one question began to pull at my soul, "Why were there so many addicts suffering in the Church. I personally witnessed what God was doing in the anonymous programs; and many of the anonymous programs didn't give God the glory. They said things like "get a God of your understanding," or "if that light is your God let it be your God." This bothered me a great deal, but I witnessed people being freed from their addictions and I couldn't deny that.

In the Church, I witnessed the power of God in the "laying on of hands." With one touch from God, I have seen people healed from this disease. On the other hand, the number of addicts and alcoholics that were being freed in the Church were small compared to those being healed in the anonymous programs. This bothered me because I knew that we served a mighty and powerful God - a God who was first in everything, first in healing, first in recovery, and first in living. I knew my God could do anything and wanted more from His church.

Deep down in my soul I knew God had put the anonymous programs together, but, somewhere down the line, they had gotten away from giving God all the glory. Growing in the Word of God, and at the same time applying the 12 steps of recovery into my life, I found that this AA program that had changed so many people's lives started in the Church. *(see The Church and Its Relationship with Alcoholics Anonymous)* God revealed to me that He wanted me to bring recovery to the Church and bring Jesus to the anonymous programs. Wow! What an order, but it wouldn't be me it would be God.

Before I started this ministry, there was one question that had to be answered: *Why is it that some addicts can have hands laid on them and be delivered from drugs and alcohol addiction and others cannot?* These are some of the answers that I received from the Church:

1. "The person laying on hands is not anointed."
2. "The person laying on hands does not have enough faith."
3. "The person receiving really does not want to receive his healing."
4. "The person receiving does not know how to receive his healing."
5. "The person receiving has a lack of faith."

I found out that some of these answers may be true especially when it pertains to the addict/alcoholic. On any given day they can want to be free and on the next day change their minds. Educating the addict/alcoholic is first. They have know what freedom looks like and how to get it, daily.

Consequently, when freedom and deliverance are not obtained for addicts/alcoholics they walk away believing:
1. God doesn't love them.
2. This God stuff is not real.
3. Why go to God.
4. Maybe there is something wrong with me, and I'll never get free.

Once again, the Bible says, *"My people perish because of a lack of knowledge."* This book will attempt help the Church and the addictive person understand Christian recovery. As I continue to study the Word and apply God's principles in my life, I realize that I have been called to God's ministry in two areas:

- Working with addicts/alcoholics - teaching them how to be free, and teaching them to understand the disease of addiction.
- Working with Churches - teaching them the process of recovery and showing them how to walk with the person who is in recovery.

Today, after 33 years in the ministry, I believe I have an answer to the question, "Why are hands laid on some addicts causing them to be delivered from drugs and alcohol addiction and others are not delivered?" Here we go:

1. Let's look at those who came to the altar and allowed the Man of God to lay hands on them and never used drugs and alcohol again. This group of now delivered addicts/alcoholics left the altar with made-up minds, willing to surrender **everything**. **The key, *they were willing* to give up everything** On that day, *they were willing* to give up the old friends, the old playgrounds, cigarettes, alcohol, drugs, and their whole lifestyle changed.
2. On the other hand, there were those who came to that same altar (to that same Man of God on that same day), left the Church and continued to drink and use. *I was in this group.* So what was the difference? This group came to the altar to be delivered from **drugs and alcohol only**. They did not come to be delivered from the lifestyle. After spending time with the addicts/alcoholics who continued to practice their disease, we found that they all had these things in common:
   - Disobedience
   - Selfishness
   - Pride
   - Denial

God hates these four character defects. These defects must be dealt with before true freedom can take place. Remember, these same four defects got Satan kicked out of heaven. *The Process of Recovery God's Plan "B"* directly deals with disobedience, selfishness, pride, and denial, along with others.

We thank God for "Plan A" which was the laying on of hands, but we also thank God for "Plan B" which is the *process of recovery*. For those who do not receive "Plan A" the laying on of hands, "Plan B" is just as powerful. We miss "Plan B" (the process of recovery) because of a lack of knowledge or because we were always looking for "Plan A".

This book is to help the Church know that there is another alternative. We that get free through God's alternate plan thank God for it, along with our family and friends. We know that the laying on of hands is real and powerful.   Our job in Christian recovery is to help them develop this faith and trust in God through simple principles that will change their lives.

JOURNEY FROM DARKNESS TO LIGHT
(Ron's Story)

Born and raised on the east side of Los Angeles, California, I grew up in a loving home with two sisters and one brother. After witnessing the Watts riots, I knew Los Angeles was a dangerous place to live but I felt well protected by my mother and father who worked hard to give our family everything we needed.

At the age of ten, my family moved to Inglewood, California. At this time, Inglewood was predominately white and was considered a very safe place to live. Yet it was in Inglewood that I had my first encounter with racism. It was in Inglewood that I found out I was different; I was black.

During my middle school years, most of the white people began to move out of the neighborhood, and African Americans began moving in. Slowly, Inglewood was being split in half. The east side of Inglewood was 70% Black, and the west side was 98% White.

In 1969, a year before I was to enroll into Morningside High School, a predominantly black high school, a law was passed that would change my life forever. The kids in our neighborhood were being bused to Inglewood High School. Inglewood High School was located on the west side, and was an all white high school.

That very first day was a day I would never forget. There were two hundred African American kids pulling up in big yellow buses to a school that had two thousand whites. White people were picketing with signs that read, "Niggers go home," parents were screaming at us as we drove up. Some of our parents arrived and verbal and physical altercations erupted. Some students got off the bus fighting, and the police took many people to jail that day. One white person argued so much that he had a heart attack and had to be rushed to the hospital while African American observers and applauded. On that day, many things changed in my life, including how I viewed the world and how close I became to the African Americans now attending the school. In the beginning, I never really wanted to go to Inglewood High; not because of any racist views, but because Morningside High had a great sports program. Now that I was faced with all this hatred, resentment and the fact that people didn't want me there, it was all the more reason for me to stay and fight against what I believed was wrong.

In the coming months, there were many debates, many fights, and many suspensions. Eventually, the physical fighting slowed down, but the confrontations continued. We had to fight for everything in those early days. We fought for the type of food was to be served on the menu, to celebrating special days in African-American history.

While this was going on at Inglewood High, there was another war brewing deep on the east and south sides of Los Angeles. Black gangs formed and young people were splitting Los Angeles into two groups. The black youth at Inglewood received news of these gangs, and found it hard to believe, especially when we were fighting racism everyday on campus.

It was 1972, when the notorious gang called the Crips crossed the line at Inglewood High and stabbed one of my best friends, Little Tex, it was at this time we knew things had to change. I remember, vividly, those days after the stabbing. Many of my friends got together to discuss Little Tex's stabbing and some of the other things that was going on with this Crip gang. It was all we talked about on campus. One day we met at a friend's house in his garage. The anger in that garage was heated and intense. Revenge was on the lips of many of the people there. We all decided to go to the hospital and visit Little Tex, and I will never forget seeing him lying in the hospital with tubes going through his body. It was on that day that my friends and I pledged our allegiance to the newly formed group in Inglewood called the "family gang" now called the Blood gang.

From 1972 to 1974, I associated myself with some guys that dedicated their lives to gang banging. I didn't live and breathe banging, many of my other friends was sports jocks so I spent a lot of time with them. I also had to keep my grades up. I feared my mother more than any gang and she didn't believe in bringing home "D's or F's", but I didn't run from altercations either. We found ourselves in gang fights, shoot-outs, robberies and hanging out with hardened criminals. Today, I know it was God who kept me from being killed, or ever going to jail.

In the family gang, I was given two names: Shot Gun Slim, Old English, and later on selling drugs they labeled me "The Brougham". They gave me the name "Shot Gun Slim" because I carried a sawed-off shotgun and I was a very skinny kid. "Old English" because I drank Old English 800 malt liquor all the time, and Brougham, in my drug dealing days, because like the Cadillac, I considered myself to be the top of the line.

To this day, I credit my mother and father for making me keep my grades up. No matter how crazy I became, I could not bring D's or F's into my parent's home. There was no bigger gang than my Mother and Father. I believe I was the only gang member that studied for tests, turned in reports, and spent time in the library- all with a .38 special in my pocket. My parents believed in the old theory, "I brought you into this world and I can take you out!"

In my last years of high school, I began to experiment with marijuana and hard liquor. Chasing women started to overrule gang banging. Most of the women I wanted to date didn't want to have anything to do with a gang banger. That was just one reason to give up banging. The other was because of my encounter with racism, and fighting for the rights of African-Americans at Inglewood High. Gang banging was something I never wanted to do, but it was something I felt I had to do if I wanted to stay alive. Those early years at Inglewood High School gave me an education like no other. The bond between the African-American students at that school was stronger than most family structures. Nobody liked us - not the whites on the inside of the school, nor the "Crips" on the outside of the school. We stuck together like glue because it was too dangerous to be caught alone.

In 1974, the last year of high school, my closest friends and I made a decision to quit banging all together. Most of us were thinking about college and what we were going to do for the rest of our lives. Everyone had his or her reasons for quitting, but mine was easy. The deep down love for my people, and most of the women that I wanted to date, didn't like gangbangers. They were educated and wanted to do something with their lives and the women in my life, my mother, aunts, sister was ladies. Some of the women I was hanging out with were gang banging and not the type of women I wanted to date.

In my last year at Inglewood High, my mother and father divorced, and that was a very hard period in my life. I didn't understand this break up; I always believed they would be together forever. After my father left, my mother struggled with taking care of three kids, and in my attempt to contribute to the household, I choose to sell marijuana. In the beginning, I looked at selling drugs as away to take care of myself and contribute to the household, but as the money got longer, bigger, and came faster, I fell in love with the power and the lifestyle. The more money I had, the more power I had, and, unbeknownst to me, these two combinations brought women, which turned out to be right up my alley.

After graduating from Inglewood High, I enrolled at El Camino Jr. College. While I was there, I continued to sell marijuana, only now on a larger scale. After a while, I began to feel that school was getting in the way of my business; so, I quit school and sold dope full time.

By the age of 20, I was selling drugs in different parts of the country and made up my mind to deal drugs for the rest of my life. By this time, I had been introduced to all types of drugs - PCP, heroin, and cocaine. Cocaine turned out to be my main source of income. By the age of 24, I had started manufacturing crack cocaine and selling it in large quantities, at the same time becoming addicted to drugs myself. By the time I was 25 years old, my habit had grown to $800 a day. I had become my best customer. After hundreds of times trying to quit on my own, the addiction began to take its toll on me. Either using drugs, or trying to get more, consumed my every waking moment. Staying up for days without sleeping or eating, I slowly began to deteriorate. At one time people called me "Big Ron." Weighting 220 pounds at 6'4'', I worked out in the gym everyday and was a fairly big guy. Now, because of my using and abusing drugs, I had withered down to 147 pounds.

In April of 1981, with the help of my family, I was able to go into a 28-day program at the Care Unit Rehabilitation Center. There I learned a lot about recovery and myself. I learned about the Anonyms program and before I left that program, I knew these programs would be a major factor for the rest of my life. That wasn't the most important piece of information that I learned in those 28 days. In the program, I met a nurse who turned out to be an angel. Her name was June Joseph and she shared Jesus with me every night. Every night, she would come into my room and share a scripture with me, and tell me to read something in the Bible. She encouraged me often by telling me everything was going to be all right if I'd only surrender to the Love of God. Since then she has gone home to be with the Lord, and I will never forget what she did for me.

After leaving that rehab, I joined a gym at one of the local parks in Inglewood and became a dedicated body builder. It was here at this gym I met some brothers who loved the Lord and they shared the Word of God with me everyday. It was in that gym that I accepted Jesus Christ as my personal Lord and Savior.

I continued my after-care program by getting involved with Narcotics Anonymous (NA) and Alcoholics Anonymous (AA). Cocaine Anonymous (CA) had not yet been formed, but today I attend those meeting as well. In these programs, I made many new friends, learned a lot about myself and how to stay free from drugs and alcohol; but none of that information compared to the relationship I had formed with my Lord and Savior.

I also stayed in contact with June, the nurse that shared the Word of God with me for the first time, and she became my prayer partner. I joined the Church she attended, Maranatha Community Church, where a friend of mine from childhood, Billy Ingram, was the pastor. I sat under that ministry for four years which was, and still is, a Word-driven church. It was at Maranatha that God first spoke to me about a Christ-centered 12 -step program for all Churches.

I presented this vision to Pastor Ingram and he allowed me to start a Christ-centered meeting called "Habit Free" on Monday nights. Addicts and alcoholics flocked to this meeting, and for the first time in my life, it felt like I was doing something right. However, there was one thing wrong with this meeting, and it had to be addressed. Addicts and alcoholics would come to the meeting on a Monday night, and by Wednesday or Saturday, many of them were getting high or drinking again. Once again God spoke to me, and told me not to "re-invent the wheel," but to copy a program that He already had in place, Alcoholics Anonymous, and bring it back to the Church *(not knowing that Alcoholics Anonymous started in the Church – see Chapter I, The Church and Its Relationship with Alcoholics Anonymous)*. God shared with me one of the reasons Alcoholics Anonymous, Narcotics Anonymous, and Cocaine Anonymous were so successful. They had meetings for the recovering person every night of the week. It was then I contacted Ronald Wright, now the Reverend Ron Wright. I heard Ron share at a NA meeting and in his pitch; he talked about how God had saved his life. Ron also belonged to a Ward AME Church that was not afraid of being on the front line. I witnessed another brother, named Rene Whitehead, sharing about the power of God and how God brought him out of his addiction. He was also attending West Angeles Church of God In Christ another front line church in the LA area.

In 1989, God led me to move my church membership to West Angeles Church of God in Christ, where Bishop Charles E. Blake is the Pastor. As head of the substance abuse department, we offer one-on-one counseling, and every Friday night our substance abuse committee holds a support group for addicts and alcoholics, and a separate family support group called Tough Love led by my wife Yolonda Simmons. We also started a Saturday women-only Free N One meeting led by Rochelle Collins.

I called these brothers together in the summer of 1988 and we formed the now nationally known organization *Free N One drug and alcohol recovery program*. Free N One's job is to set up meetings in churches all over the nation. Pastors and church leaders are calling from all over the country, wanting more information about Free N One. Not long after starting God's Free N One program, we noticed that we were missing a very important component that was needed in the ministry, something for the family members. God allowed us to see that the addict or the alcoholic was now being freed from his bondage, but the family member who had stood by them had also been tremendously affected by his usage and needed help. It was then that we started a support meeting called Free N One's "Tough Love". In these meetings the family members who have been emotionally, and sometimes physically abused, slowly learn to let God put his/her lives back together through God's Word and support from other co-dependents.

In 1991, Bishop Charles E. Blake asked me to head the First Jurisdiction of Southern California COGIC (Church of God in Christ) Transition House and to set up a policy for the 250 churches in our jurisdiction. This house is a 10-bed facility for men who require more meetings and support, and need to remove themselves from their current environment in order to get well. The success of Transition House has been nothing short of a miracle. Men are finding freedom and turning their lives over to Jesus.

I later returned to UCLA and received a certificate in drug and alcohol counseling, and another certificate for alcohol and drug studies.

On April 22, 2014, I celebrated 33 years of being drug and alcohol free. I am married to my wife for life, Yolonda Simmons. We have three children, the twins Daniel and Danyell, 34, and Quianna, 31. I have eight grand children: Isaiah, Autum, Ndey, Cash, Brice, Sadee, Anderson and Hunter.

THE CHURCH

For years the Church has been the first line of defense for a person who is suffering from any sickness. The Church is always praying and caring for people who are overcome by sickness and disease. Today I thank God for those that prayed for people like me. It was their prayers that have me here today.

In the 1940's, and 50's, before anyone knew alcohol was a disease, the Church knew something was desperately wrong and fought against the legalization of buying and selling alcohol. In the 50's and 60's, when Satan attacked this country with marijuana, hallucinogenic drugs, and uppers and downers, the church spoke against drug and alcohol usage. In the 70's, 80's and 90's, the Church was there, helping where they could and standing up for what was right.

Today we are able to see Satan's offensive plan of attack. The strategy is to attack each major city and let the problem filter down to the suburbs and to the farmlands. There isn't a place in this country that has not been affected by this disease called addiction. In the African American community, Satan attacks the head of the family (the male) knowing that the rest will soon fall.

So what is the Church's response to this attack? In the Bible we see that God shows out when impossible shows up. In other words, a miracle can't show up until impossible is present. Because of what Satan is doing in our communities, we are just right for a miracle. It is time we take this battle to another level and win this war in the name of Jesus! Part of this answer can be found in the Great Commission, *Mark 16:15-18: "And Jesus said to them, "Go into all the world and preach the gospel to every creature. (16) He who believes and is baptized will be saved; but he who does not believe will be condemned, (17) And these signs will follow those who believe: In My name they will cast out demons; they will speak with new tongues; (18) they will take up serpents; and if they drink anything deadly, it will by no means hurt them; they will lay hands on the sick, and they will recover."*

We in the Church know that people can be delivered with one touch from God. Unfortunately, some individuals in the Church believe this is the only way to recover. If this were so, we should be able to go to every state, to every city, to every dope house, back alley and bar, and deliver people from this disease called addiction. Does God have another plan to help His people or does Satan win this battle? God forbid! Believe me there is a plan that will work.

It is a proven fact that some people are instantly delivered by God's power, never to go and use or drink again. Then there are other addicts/alcoholics who have the same hands laid on them, then turn right around and continue to be ruled by their disease. This person wants freedom just as much as other people but for some unknown reason is unable to receive deliverance. This person needs to be educated in the area of the disease of addiction.

Let's take a look at those addicts/alcoholics who experience the miracle of deliverance by having hands laid on them and never go back to their addiction. What keeps them free, or what are they doing differently that keeps them from never going back to using or abusing drugs or alcohol?

We that work closely in this ministry have noticed one thing. The addicts/alcoholics that come to the altar and are completely delivered--surrendered all. They are willing to give up everything.   Not only delivered from the drugs and alcohol, but the cigarettes, lying, cheating, stealing, and fornication. They are ***willing*** to give up their so-called friends and the whole lifestyle**.**   When freedom takes place, the power of God moves in them and, in most cases, the desire for this lifestyle leaves as well. The key is being ***willing***, willing to surrender all, with a made up mind to serve God.

Now on the other hand, addicts/alcoholics who go to that same altar but return to using and drinking go to the altar just to be delivered from the drugs and alcohol. They are not ***willing*** to change their lifestyle, just the drinking and using. God, who knows their heart, will not let freedom take place. Freedom is surrender and release.

Because of a lack of knowledge and education on the part of the Church and their inexperience in the process of recovery, they have not been effective in this area. Even though the addict/alcoholic is thoroughly convinced he/she wants to quit, but "want" is not enough to keep them free. *Matthew 26:41 says, "The spirit is indeed willing, but the flesh is weak."* From the pews, to the choir stand, to the usher board, to the pulpit, untreated addicts/alcoholics are occupying Churches all over the world. Two myths have infiltrated the Church:

1. "He stopped so he must be okay." - Because he has stopped drinking and using for a few months, does not mean that he is healed. This demon will wait patiently until the unsuspecting person has his guards down, then the demon will attack. *1 Peter 5: 8 says," Satan is like a roaring lion, seeking who he might devour."* Matthew 12:43-45 says, *"When an unclean spirit goes out of a man, he goes through dry places, seeking rest, and finds none. 44Then he says, 'I will return to my house from which I came.' And when he comes, he finds it empty, swept, and put in order. 45Then he goes and takes with him seven other spirits more wicked than himself, and they enter and dwell there; and the last state of that man is worse than the first. So shall it also be with this wicked generation."*

2. "If we can just get them a job." - The answer to their problem is not a job. Most addicts and alcoholics have skills and are employable. The problem is "pay day," the day they receive their check. Money is the #1 trigger to the recovering person.

Traditionally the Church will go overboard in helping someone who has confessed to having a problem with drugs or alcohol and treat them with kid gloves. The Church, or someone in the Church, will take care of the immediate needs, which is okay. The problem begins when the Church continues to take care of this person and does not allow them to take care of themselves, or trust God for themselves. (Getting him a job, finding a place to stay, making decisions, picking them up and taking them to Church and Bible studies are all good supports.) Being responsible is what most addict/alcoholics lack. If you continue taking care of their every need, they never learn to trust God for themselves. Remember, you are talking about a person who went to any length to drink and use. So they need to take that same intensity and channel it towards their recovery and their walk to sobriety in Christ. They need to go to any length to stay clean and sober. In their attempt to show love to the recovering person, the Church is enabling this person, by not allowing them to stand up for themselves. (Note: Every case is different, so you must use sound judgment and wisdom. Like the mother bird that pushes the baby bird out of the nest, we must learn how and when to let go and push.)

One of the biggest mistakes made by the Church while working with an addict/alcoholic is the assumption that he or she is well. Just because an addict/alcoholic accepts Jesus Christ as their personal Lord and Savior, this does not mean they are delivered from their addiction. With good intentions, someone in the Church tells the recovering person that they are free. When addicts start to believe they are well, they stop going to recovery meetings, checking in with their sponsor, and stops working on themselves. Remember the definition of Recovery is "Renewing the Mind" and you can't do this over night. Once they start believing they are free, they let their guards down and Satan begins his attack. The disease of addiction re-infects the addicted because they have stopped taking their medicine.   Just like any other untreated disease, addiction is alive and well and is the beginning of another bought with their drug of choice.

We don't suggest a person get too involved with operations in the church, or heavily involved in auxiliaries. A person that is just beginning this new life without any mind-altering chemical must experience the ups and downs of life before adding the pressures of ministry and other responsibilities to their plate. Learning how to live free takes time! Successful recovery recommends that a person be free from their addiction for at least six months before joining the choir, working on the usher board or any auxiliary in the Church. A recovering person who is considering holding any office, such as Elder or Deacon, or ministering to anyone in the congregation, should wait a year. When it comes to handling monies we suggest 1 year with a job. This gives the person time to find out who they are, and whose they are in Christ. It also gives them time to go through life's difficulties without using or drinking. During this time, a stronger foundation can be built in the Lord.

In the past, we have seen too many Christians with an untreated disease confessing before men and the congregation that God had freed them from their addiction. However, because they have never addressed their behaviors associated the disease of addiction and they stopped doing the things that helped them to stay free; the sickness returns and somewhere down the line they secretly go back to participating in their disease. For those who are singing in the choir, working on the usher board, or sitting in the pulpit, the embarrassment is too great. Because of pride, they cannot tell anyone about this fall because they have already confessed before men that God has set them free. Therefore, they try their best to hide their drinking and using until they cannot hide it any longer. Most of the time, an addicted person will disappear from Church without a trace, only to reappear at another Church to go through the same cycle.

Some addict/alcoholics blame God, but most of them feel that they have let God down or let the Church down. Some believe that God is angry with them because they have failed again, and they start believing that this freedom will never happen for them. It is crucial that the Church and the recovering person never forget that they are sick people with an illness and it is going to take time to get well.

The Church must learn how to be patient with that person who has just entered into this new walk called recovery. Give them time to grow up before adding responsibilities to their lives.

So how do you work with a person who has been involved in the Church most of their life and is still struggling with drugs and alcohol addiction? He has sung in the choir, has been on the Jr. Deacon board, and then on the Deacon board. He knows everyone in the Church and everyone knows him. He has taught Bible studies and led revivals. What do you say to a person who already has a personal relationship with God?   How do you convince him that Jesus is the way to his freedom in Christ?   He will tell you that he has been praying and fasting, going from one revival to another and attending all types of healing service. He has been dipped in water, covered in oil, but he continues to use. What is your answer to him?

First, you have to separate their involvement with "church". Most of the time, they look at all the work they do in church and think that this will fix them. Even those around them believe they are doing well because of their involvement, but their commitment to holiness and righteous is weak. They lead a double life. At church things are great, but, at home, they are caught up in un-godly behaviors. Second, this type of addict/alcoholic actually has the same problem as the addict that does not know God. **PRIDE** is their biggest problem. Because of who they think they are, and how they are supposed to act in the Church, they find it hard to ask for help. Humbling themselves before family and friends seems impossible. If confronted they deny or water down the problem.

Next they have to surrender to a faith-base support group such as Free N One. Here they will begin to learn and apply the tool that is needed to stay free from their addiction. They have to obtain a sponsor (see chapter on sponsors) someone with at least one year clean and sober and a working knowledge of the steps and the process of recovery. If they are still willing to be involved in auxiliaries or ministries in the church, those leaders have every right to get to communicate with that sponsor and updated on the recovering persons progress. Sponsors recommend it.

We discourage close friends, others in the ministry that know nothing about the process of recovery. Without a working knowledge of the process of recovery it is easy for the recovering person to manipulate those that don't understand.

Today we see too many people who have been injured by people in the church with good intentions. *Hosea 4:6 says, My people parish from a lack of knowledge".* Educating ourselves on Codependency, The Process of Recovery, The Disease of Addiction and the Enabling process is a must for all churches. People come to the church for help and we should provide them with the best.

In one case, a Pastor's daughter who was struggling with a very serious crack cocaine addiction told me that she did not want another saint to lay hands on her, sprinkle oil on her or dip her in water. Today, this sister is clean and sober ten years through the grace of God and the process of recovery. It is time the Church takes a look at this process called Recovery. God ordains this process, which comes right out of the Word of God.

The Church should be the first place a person goes for help. When they arrive, there should be a program in place that is highly successful. The Bible says at Matthew 11:28, *"Come unto me all you who labor and are heavy laden and I will give you rest."* God will send them, and when they arrive we have to be prepared to receive them. Education is the key to the Church's success. From the pulpit to the congregation, the Church and the practicing addict/alcoholic should understand that:

- the disease of addiction is a sickness; and
- the practicing addicts/alcoholics aren't bad people trying to be good but sick people trying to get well.

The Church should be a safe place for any recovering addict/alcoholic to learn how to be free. However, if they feel people are going to belittle them or talk about them behind their backs, why should they go? The Bible also says at James 5:16, *"Confess your faults one to another and pray one for another that ye may be healed. The effectual fervent prayer of a righteous man availeth much."* Can someone bring their deepest darkest secrets to you and it goes no further than you? Secrets that haunt their every waking moment that causes them to drink and use? Is there a safe place in the church for people to share the hurts and pains of life?

We teach that the Church is a spiritual hospital where sick people come to get well. Most addicts that love the Lord run from the Church because of shame, a sense of failure, guilt, or embarrassment. Most of them disappear from the Church, with their disease still untreated, and they wander hopelessly letting the disease consume them fully.

For years recovering people that came out of secular programs such as Alcoholics Anonymous, Narcotics Anonymous, and Cocaine Anonymous were taught to refer to themselves as addicts/alcoholics. This was considered against God's teaching in the Church, and they were told not to confess being an addict or alcoholic. The Church would take them to II Corinthians 5:17, *"Therefore if anyone is in Christ he is a new creation old things have passed away behold all things have become new."* Because this scripture is not fully explained to the addict/alcoholic, most of them will hear this and try their best to live in freedom and not confess that they are recovering addicts/alcoholics. When their disease overwhelms them and they begin drinking and using again, they leave the Church crushed and embarrassed. They feel less than Christians and defeated. Some even question if they are still Christians.

When we use II Corinthians 5:17, *"Therefore if anyone is in Christ he is a new creation old things have passed away behold all things have become new;"* teachers in the Church must let the recovering person know that Paul was talking about the **spirit of man** becoming new. The flesh is still weak. It will take time for the flesh to catch up with this new spirit. The process of recovery, prayer, fasting, and always keeping your addiction before you, (so you don't forget) will be the tools you will use to bring the flesh under submission.

It is the recovering person's responsibility to replace the old with something new. That something new is the Word of God, through the process of recovery. (Not just knowing the Word but living the Word of God.) This process of recovery is not going to happen overnight. It takes time to become new in the flesh, especially when you are working with alcoholics/addicts. They tend to hold on to the "old" because they are comfortable with the old. Even if the "old" almost destroyed them. We in the Church must understand that addicts and alcoholics did not become addicts overnight. The disease progressively got worse.

Still today, one of the first places an addict or alcoholic looks for freedom from this disease is the Church. Deep down inside in the midst of all the madness that comes with the hell of drinking and using, most addicts and alcoholics will cry out to God when they can't take it any more.

As the Church comes together as one, equipped with knowledge and understanding about the disease of addiction, and the process of recovery, we will defeat this monster that is plaguing our communities.

If the Pastor supports recovery from the pulpit, their Church becomes a safe place for the addicted person. It becomes easier to ask for help when the Pastor shares from the podium about God's recovery.

When the Church only teaches freedom and not how to get this freedom, the addict/alcoholic hides in the closet, always wondering what is wrong with him.

WHAT WE BELIEVE

We believe that alcohol and drug addictions are symptoms of sinful behavior and negative emotions. We believe persons using drugs/alcohol and the love ones that are affected by their using must find freedom. We believe that this freedom is found in establishing a personal relationship with Jesus Christ and living His Word. We believe that the Church will lead the battle in the war against drug and alcohol addiction, once the Church has been trained in the area of recovery. We believe drugs and alcohol addiction crosses denominational lines so denominations must band together to win this battle. We believe that family members and loved ones are deeply affected by the addicted person's behavior and recovery must take place. We believe that this is a winnable war!

THE CHURCH AND ITS RELATIONSHIP WITH ALCOHOLICS ANONYMOUS

Confronting the Church concerning a weakness in *any* area can be considered dangerous by most. However, if we, "the Church," want to take this battle to the next level and win this war on drug and alcohol addiction, we must take an honest look at ourselves, and how we battle addiction. As Christians We believe in Jesus, we believe in the "Lion of Judah" The King of Kings and the Lord of Lords. He is the First the Last, Alpha and Omega. Why are we, "The Church," loosing this war against drugs and alcohol addiction? "The church" that is rooted and grounded in the Word of God and looks to and believes Christ for everything. The heartbeat of our community, "the Church", a place where lives are changed, the blind see, the death hear, but in this war against drugs and alcohol addiction we're losing.

When God calls us to ministry whatever it might be lives should change because of the services rendered. People will be healed, delivered and set free and most importantly people will accept Jesus Christ as Lord.

The Bible say's *my people perish because of a lack of knowledge*." Understanding how to attack what Satan is doing through addiction is key. Renewing the mind with spiritual tools will be the key to victory.

In some neighborhoods, there is a church on every corner and enough junkies and alcoholics in these neighborhoods to fill every church. These are just a few questions that have to be asked by Christians who believe. Why are we losing this war on drugs and alcohol? Do we win this war? Or do we continue doing what we have been doing (losing), acting as if this problem is really not that bad, looking the other way, hoping it will get better?

So today we take time out in this chapter to look at one of the most successful programs know to man, Alcoholics Anonymous and the 12 Steps to Recovery. These 12 Steps have helped more addicts and alcoholic than any program on the face of this earth.

The first question asked is what are they doing that is working so well? What I am about to share with you will open the eyes of most Christians, along with those who are rooted in the Anonymous program and others who continue to stumble in the dark, losing a winnable war! We are going to take a quick look at the founders of Alcoholic Anonymous and their relationship with the church.

Bill Wilson Story

Better known as Bill W.

Accounts taken fromHistory of Alcoholics Anonymous - Wikipedia,
and Washington Post Obituary of Bill Wilson - Serenity Found

Bill Wilson was an alcoholic who had ruined a promising career on <u>Wall Street</u> by his drinking. He also failed to graduate from law school because he was too drunk to pick up his diploma. His drinking damaged his marriage, and he was hospitalized for alcoholism at Towns Hospital four times in 1933-1934 under the care of <u>Dr. William Silkworth</u>. On Wilson's first stay at Towns Hospital, Dr. Silkworth explained to him his theory that alcoholism is an illness rather than a moral failure or failure of willpower. Silkworth believed that alcoholics were suffering from a mental obsession, combined with an allergy that made compulsive drinking inevitable, and to break the cycle one had to completely abstain from alcohol use. Wilson was elated to find that he suffered from an illness, and he managed to stay off alcohol for a month before he resumed drinking.

When Ebby Thacher visited Wilson at his New York apartment and told him "he had got religion," Wilson's heart sank. Until then, Wilson had struggled with the existence of God, but of his meeting with Thacher he wrote: "My friend suggested what then seemed a novel idea. He said, 'Why don't you choose your own conception of God?' That statement hit me hard. It melted the icy intellectual mountain in whose shadow I had lived and shivered many years. I stood in the sunlight at last." When Thacher left, Wilson continued to drink. Thacher returned a few days later bringing with him Shep Cornell, another Oxford member who was aggressive in his tactics of promoting the Oxford Program, but despite their efforts Wilson continued to drink.

The next morning Wilson arrived at Calvary Rescue Mission in a drunken state looking for Thacher. Once there, he attended his first Oxford Group meeting, where he answered the call to come to the altar and, along with other penitents, gave his life to Christ. Wilson excitedly told his wife Lois about his spiritual progress, yet the next day he drank again and a few days later readmitted himself to Towns Hospital for the fourth and last time.

Mr. Wilson went into a New York City hospital and was detoxified - but fell into a severe depression:

"Finally it seemed to me as though I were at the very bottom of the pit," he later wrote. "All at once I found myself crying out, 'If there is a God, let him show himself! I am ready to do anything, anything!'"

"Suddenly the room lit up with a great white light. It seemed to me, in the mind's eye, that I was on a mountain and that a wind, not of air, but of spirit was blowing. And then it burst upon me that was a free man. "I thought to myself, 'So this is the God of the preachers'" Bill Wilson never took another drink!

Upon his release from the hospital on December 18, 1934, Wilson moved from the Calvary Rescue Mission to the Oxford meetings at Calvary House. There Wilson socialized after the meetings with other ex-drinking Oxfords and became interested in learning how to help other alcoholics achieve sobriety. It was during this time that Wilson went on a crusade to save alcoholics. Sources for his prospects were the Calvary Rescue Mission and Towns Hospital. But of all the alcoholics Wilson tried to help, not one stayed sober.

Dr. Bob

Accounts from the book <u>Dr. Bob and the Good Old Timers</u>.

This is the official account of Dr. Bob's life leading up to his historic meeting with Bill Wilson. (Dr. Bob and Bill Wilson founded Alcoholics Anonymous.) This book goes into detail about this historical meeting between two alcoholics that took helping alcoholics to another level. Also, it goes into detail about how they were introduced to the biblical principles that have changed so many lives, and are still changing lives today.

The Oxford Group

The Oxford Group was a group of Christians founded by Frank Buchman in 1921. Members of the Oxford Group sought to achieve spiritual regeneration by surrendering to God through rigorous self-examination, confessing their character defects to other human beings, making restitution for harm done to others, and giving without thought of reward.

Emphasis was placed on prayer and on seeking guidance from God in all matters. The movement also relied on the study of the Scriptures.

The core of the program was the "four absolutes:" absolute honesty, unselfishness, purity and love. These four absolutes were the beginning of the 12 Steps to Recovery and are still published and widely quoted at A.A. meetings in the Akron-Cleveland area, where A.A was founded.

The Oxford Group also practiced the five "C's" and the "five procedures." The five C's were confidence, confession, conviction, conversion, and continuance. The five procedures were: give in to God, listen to God's direction, check guidance, restitution and sharing for witness and for confession.

The Oxford Group began its meetings in homes in the Akron area. It was there Dr. Bob began to soak up the spiritual and religious philosophies of the ages, and was impressed because "they seemed very much at ease." However, even with all of this, Bob still got drunk.

It was April of 1935 when a couple of Oxford Groupers got together and asked what were they going to do about Dr. Bob and his drinking problem. Mind you, none of these groupers were alcoholics.

Therefore, they planned a special meeting and came to a conclusion. The reason they were not reaching Dr. Bob was that the groupers themselves were not being completely honest about what was going on in their lives. In this historical meeting, every grouper shared their shortcomings and secrets. Once everyone finished they all turned to Bob who said, "Well, you good people have all shared things that I am sure were very costly to you, and I am going to tell you something which may cost me my profession. I am a secret drinker and I can't stop." Thus, the birth of the first Alcoholics Anonymous meeting!

Although arguments have been, and will be made, for other significant occasions in A.A. history, it is generally agreed that Alcoholics Anonymous began there in Akron, on June 10, 1935. (p 75).

Bill and Bob Leave the Oxford Group

The Oxford Group continued to grow, mainly because of the large number of alcoholics that were now coming to these meetings. In some cases, they would start the meeting together and later split up. The Oxford Group would take the large room and the A.A. members would take the smaller room. Slowly this changed and became a problem for the non-drinking Oxford Group members. The A.A. members began to get more vocal and this posed a problem for the Oxford Group.

In 1939, Clarence S. became very involved in the A.A. portion of the Oxford Group and was drawing in alcoholics from all over. Many of them were Catholic whose doctrine clashed with the Oxford Group. On May 11, 1939, Clarence S. made the announcement at the Oxford Group meeting that this was the last time the Cleveland alcoholic members would meet with the non-drinking Oxford Group members. (p 164)

These were very hard times for both groups. Choosing sides made it hard on everyone. Other Oxford/A.A. groups weren't so quick to separate because of loyalty. However, the inevitable was going to happen. This was bigger than the Oxford Group, and the world was looking for a cure for alcoholism.

Free N One Puts Christ back into the Program

No one would dare argue that the "Anonymous" program is the most successful program on the face of the earth today. The lists of anonymous programs are endless. Alcohol, Narcotic, Cocaine, Emotional, Gamblers, Sex, Meth, and countless others are changing lives daily. The 12 steps and the process of recovery are considered a miracle to millions.

We too thank God for the Oxford Group and the pioneers that started this life changing program but there is one problem. Satan could care less about a person being free from an addiction. Addiction is just a smoke screen for is ultimate goal and that is for people not to accept Christ as Lord and Savior. Of course Satan would love for a person to be addicted and tormented here on earth and eventually spend the rest of eternity in damnation. But if he had to release one it would be freedom from addiction.

We in Free N One believe that you can be free from both. Freedom from addiction and free to accept Christ as Lord and Savior and spend the rest of your life with Christ. Why not have them both!

We have taken those same 12 steps and the process of recovery back to the Church from which they came. We've learned from the Oxford Group and vowed not to let politics or religion separate what God has started.

We clearly understand that God can deliver a person from addiction with one touch. That's God's plan "A". God's plan "B" is the Process of Recovery and the 12 Steps!

Chapter II

WELCOME TO RECOVERY

RECOVERY IS ABOUT CHANGE

In order for a complete change to come about in your life you must be willing to change. Pray that these questions will penetrate the will of man that misguided you to this point today. Remember, you must **surrender to win or the way up is down.** You were doing your best thinking when you ended up hooked on drugs or alcohol. Be willing to take suggestions and listen to those that have walked the path you are attempting to walk. And never forget, "When there is no change, there is no change."

WELCOME TO RECOVERY

The first half of this book will introduce you to recovery. This information will help you understand who you are and why you do what you do. It will answer those questions that you have asked yourself for years.

It will also give you a starting place and point you in the right direction towards a freedom that will be reachable one day, one-step at a time.

Rarely have we seen someone fail that followed these Godly principles.

"My People Parish For A Lack Of Knowledge"

THE DISEASE OF ADDICTION & THE ADDICT/ALCOHOLIC

By the time most addicts or alcoholics realize they have problems, they are mentally exhausted, physically destroyed, and spiritually bankrupt. This is caused by countless attempts to stop drinking and using, and always returning to the same old lifestyle. Often they return, drinking and using more than before.

Alcoholism and drug addiction are considered a disease by most major medical associations in the world today. Continued drinking or continued substance abuse characterizes this illness. It is very important that the recovering person recognize that he or she has a disease a sickness. We can't stress this enough.

So why is this important? The fight becomes easier when a person surrenders to the fact that we are sick people trying to get well, instead of bad people trying to be good. A person who understands he or she is sick can now start taking the correct medicines to be healed. Once a recovering person understands and accepts the fact that they are sick, they can start seeking treatment for their illness. It should be reiterated, that like any other disease, if left untreated, the disease of alcoholism or addiction would only worsen. One reason most addicts/alcoholics struggle so long is many believe they can return to sociable drinking and using. The line between social drinking and alcoholism is a very fine, invisible line. One may not realize that once you cross that "fine, invisible line" into addiction or alcoholism, there is no turning back to sociable drinking and using. The disease gets progressively worse every time you take a drink or a hit. Every person's "invisible line" is different. Some can drink or use more than others before they cross the line. Some will drink or use for years and then some will drink or use for only months or weeks, before they cross the line. One thing we do know is once it is crossed you can't turn back. It is evident that at one time in a person's life they could drink and put the drink down or say no, because they didn't want anymore. However, one day they couldn't put the drink down and they needed another, and another, and another. One day they couldn't say no to any offers because something inside them was broken. Now when they take a drink or use drugs they want, or in most cases, need more.

The disease causes a craving beyond mental control; no matter what defense a person tried many return to abusing alcohol and drugs. Some will try changing their choice of drug or alcohol. They believe that by changing to a so-called lesser substance, the problem would be fixed. The cocaine or heroin addict would change to marijuana, and the scotch or hard drinker will change to drinking beer or wine, only to find out that this does not fix their problems, but to enhance their need to return to the drug or alcohol of their choice.

Some addicts or alcoholics make desperate attempts to stop using by blaming the people in their immediate circle or area in which they live. So they move from neighborhood to neighborhood, city to city, or state to state running from what they think is the problem, only to find out that they cannot run from themselves. We that are in recovery call this "doing a geographic." One writer wrote, "Everywhere you go, there you are." A friend of mine shared with me that he went to Africa to volunteer his time as a doctor; he had been having problems with his son experimenting with marijuana and this really concerned him. He thought this experience would be good for him and his son would look at life different. When he returned after two months, I asked him how his son did in Africa. He told me not very good, he found the dope dealer in Africa. The untreated disease was within him and will always be within him until he starts treating the illness. Once again, everywhere you go, there you are!

Once a recovering person understands he is ill, he can begin taking the right prescription or medicine that will relieve him of the pain and aggravation he or she is experiencing. When ministering to recovering addicts/alcoholics, they have to begin taking their medicine. No one will be able to take this medicine for them, no one will be there to remind them to take this medicine, and they have to want this healing on their own.

Even though addiction is a disease, most people regard it differently from any other diseases. There is pity for a person that has cancer, but for an addict or alcoholic there is anger, resentment and frustration. Some think because they brought it upon themselves, they should live with the choices they made. Others believe that they should just stop and this problem will go away. Unfortunately, it's not that easy. This sickness has to be confronted and dealt with before freedom will come.

For every sickness there is a cause. In recovery, we look for the cause and center our medication towards that cause. The causes of high blood pressure are the foods we eat, the stress of life, and lack of exercise. Addiction is a spiritual disease that centers in our mind, caused by disobedience to God's Word and a need to satisfy the flesh. This is why the Bible says we must *"renew the mind." Romans 12:2 And do not be conformed to this world, but be transformed by the renewing of your mind.* The battle to get high is fought in your mind. The Word of God changes your mind. Books like this changes your mind. Attending support group meetings and fellowshipping with people whose goal is to stay clean and sober will change your mind.

At Ephesians 4:23 says, *"I say then Walk in the Spirit, and you shall not fulfill the lust of the flesh."* Galatians 5:17-18 *says, "For the flesh lusts against the Spirit, and Spirit against the flesh; and these are contrary to one another, so you do not do the things that you wish."* This tells us that there is a major war going on inside every person. There is the spirit man that wants to do right, and the fleshly man that wants to do wrong.

Many addicts/alcoholics begin with being addicted to "more", more money, more men, more women, more drama, more things, more this more that. Drugs and alcohol is just the substance that brings pain and aggravation in their lives to the point they now need help. If dealt with correctly the drugs and alcohol can become a blessing. It can run a person right into the arms of God. However, if it is not addressed in the right manner, the addicted person is overcome by Satan's devices and they lose the war. The Bible says that, *"Satan has come to kill steal and destroy."*

The Word of God lets us know there are character flaws in every human being. *"No man is perfect, no, not one."* For the addict or alcoholic, there are two flaws that stand out and must be addressed by anyone working with recovering people. Two flaws that fuel the continued usage and attacks the flesh of man, rendering them helpless until they either surrender to God or they are destroyed by their continued practice. These two flaws are "pride and selfishness." The same pride that got Satan kicked out of heaven is what keeps the addict or alcoholic blinded from seeing the devastation in their life. Pride tells them,

"It's not that bad" or I can stop when I want too." They deny the severity of their actions, even though everyone around them recognizes the problem and are certain this person needs professional help.

Selfishness then takes over, disregarding the evidence and they defend their actions. "This is my life or Its my life I do what I want to do". By this time their sickness worsens and they continue using and drinking as if they are running out of drugs or alcohol. The more they use the more the disease grows inside. They stop caring about anyone and everyone, neglecting responsibility and destroying everything and everyone around them.

When it comes to the back sliding Christian, the road back to freedom can be harder. Those that know the Lord and have developed a relationship with Him say things like: "I don't need a recovery program, meetings, or counseling, I'll just return back to Church and attend Bible studies." Therefore, they lean unto their own understanding trying to fix themselves. Most of the time, these are the first to return to drinking and using.

As the addict/alcohol slowly falls from grace and comes to grip with their problem, selfishness keeps them from surrendering and seeking help. Selfishness yells from the rooftop, "It's my thing; I do what I want to do." They believe if they are only hurting themselves, no one else should worry about what they do. As we all know, everyone that cares about them hurts as they watch their loved ones destroy their lives. For every person addicted to drugs or alcohol there are at least 10 loved ones that are affected.

The Bible tells a story about a man that loved the Lord with all his heart, but because of his conceit, he was afflicted by an illness. II Corinthians 12:7-10 -- *"To keep me from becoming conceited because of these surpassingly great revelations, there was given me a thorn in my flesh, the messenger of Satan, to torment me. (8) Three times, I pleaded with the Lord to take it away from me. (9) But he said to me, 'My Grace is sufficient for thee, for my strength is made perfect in weakness.' Therefore I will boast all the more gladly about my weaknesses, so "that the power of Christ may rest up on me. 10) That is why, for Christ's sake, I delight in weaknesses, in insults, in hardships, in persecutions, in difficulties. For when I am weak I am strong."*

There are two quick things that we need to recognize here in this passage of scripture. First, we know this thorn was not a "rose bush thorn" piercing his flesh. Second, God didn't give Paul the thorn. God allowed Satan to give him the thorn because of Paul's conceit (spiritual disobedience). You can safely say that God allowed this affliction to happen to get Paul's attention. Some historians believe this thorn was an illness, but since we do not know what type of illness it was, for the sake of argument, let us say it was a spiritual illness or some form of addiction. Paul asked three times for the thorn to be taken away, but God said, *"My Grace is sufficient for you."* What does this mean God's grace is sufficient for you? Is God saying, "I'm not going to take the thorn away from you but you will be alright?"

Let's take a look at this picture. Here is Paul, a true man of God, and a man who wrote thirteen (13) books of the Bible while suffering from an illness. Paul asked God to relieve him of this affliction, not once, but three times. How many times did you ask God to take your addiction away? We are the same as Paul. We asked God to remove the thorn three times but God did not honor this prayer the way we wanted Him too. His response is, "My grace is sufficient for you." So many times Christians ask God to relieve them of this disease of addiction, but for most addicts and alcoholics the addiction is never taken away. Is the addiction too much for God? NO WAY! The problem with Paul was not the thorn in his flesh but the conceit that brought it on. The reason addicts and alcoholic continue to fall to their addiction, even when they have made up their minds to stop, is they are fighting against the wrong thing. Instead of fighting against the pride, selfishness and disobedience in their lives, they fight against the drugs or alcohol, or the thorn in the side. Drug and alcohol addiction is only the symptom to a greater problem.

All through the Word of God, we see God delivering people from physical aliments, helping the blind to see, the lame to walk, and the leapers to be cleansed. Rarely do you see God deliver a person from being prideful, or from selfishness, or just out right evil. What God did in this case and for many addicts and alcoholics was get their attention by allowing this thorn (drug and alcohol addiction) in their lives.

Working in the field of recovery, we find that the biggest battle for the Christian that is trying to be free can sometimes even be a harder battle to win because of what they know or think they know.   Growing up in a Christian environment where they have been filled with the Word of God, many are led astray and get caught up in drug and alcohol addiction. Some are able to achieve sobriety, (or some form of sanity) never to return to that lifestyle. However, there are others that return to God and to the Church who never become completely free. They start with good intentions to surrender to the Word of God but somewhere along the way, they fall back into the lifestyle of using and abusing. Their constant relapse tears them apart because of knowledge of the Word of God deep down inside them. When they are approached with the "process of recovery", they fight this process believing that they will be delivered with one touch from God. In actuality, they are "leaning to their own understanding."

God reserves the right to deliver whom, when, and how he wants to, and we the ones seeking help can't pick the vehicle in which God wants to heal us. For many Christians that are struggling with an addiction, the "recovery process" is God's vehicle to freedom. In the midst of their disease denial gets stronger. Therefore, they continue to use drug and alcohol, slowly disappearing from their home Church. They begin to jump from Church to Church trying to find that right Word or right minister that will deliver them from their bondage. Eventually they disappear from the church all together, surrendering to their disease.   There are three things that eventually happen to a person that lives in denial; jails, institutions or death.

For those that surrender toe the Process of Recovery discover that the disease of addiction and alcoholism lies dormant inside the recovering person, like a monster that has been locked down and arrested.   Just like the thorn stayed with Paul. The Bible never says that God took the thorn from Paul. It is the grace of God that keeps a person free. It has been documented that for addicts and alcoholics who return to drinking and using after years of freedom, feel as if they had never stopped drinking or using.   The pain, the agony, the fear and the guilt return as if they had never left. When a person returns to using, he/she frees the monster that had been locked down and it will continue destroying the now practicing addict/alcoholic. The Bible relates in II Peter 2:22, *"it's like a dog returning to his own vomit."*

When God said, "My grace is sufficient for you," He was saying, I am not taking this affliction from you, but it is my power that is keeping you from the pain and suffering that it can cause. It is my grace that is giving you peace, and in order to stay free from the pain, you must surrender all to me daily. In Paul's it was his conceit, self-importance, pride, arrogance that led to the thorn in the first place.

So in II Corinthians 12: 9-10, like Paul, *"I will boast all the more gladly about my weakness [*the thorn or disease is still with him*] so that Christ's power may rest on me. (10) That is why "for Christ's sake," I delight in weaknesses, in insults, in hardships, persecutions, in difficulties, for when I am weak, I am strong."*

In verse 9, Paul learns how to give his problem over; resting in the fact that God will take care of the problem. He has found so much comfort that he now boasts gladly about it! Paul boasts about the thorn in his flesh that caused his affliction. During this process, Paul is given a revelation and at verse 10, Paul delights in everything that is supposed to keep him down or destroy him. He recognizes that when he stops fighting and surrenders, God's power now rests on him. The Word goes on to say, for when he is weak, then and only then, does he become strong.

So don't let anyone tell you that you are not a recovering addict or alcoholic. Today, it's okay to say that you are a recovering, delivered, redeemed, blessed and happy alcoholic/addict. If anyone has any questions, just lead them to this chapter concerning Paul's thorn.

Some people in the Church will never understand this concept because they refuse to accept the fact that God said "no" to Paul and never took the thorn away! Unfortunately, it takes a near death experience or bondage, such as alcoholism or drug addiction, to understand what God is saying here. When I humble myself, I recognize I have no power to fight this bondage. Then God say's "good, finally, I have all power."

So the next question asked is, why would a person that has separated himself from this lifestyle of addiction return to such bondage? Let's explore a few of the reasons people become re-addicted or relapse.

The recovering person steps out of God's will by allowing pride and ego to rise in his/her life again. In the beginning of this road to recovery, they humbled themselves because of the pain and suffering of an addictive lifestyle. They were willing to do whatever it took to stay free. Making support group meetings, Bible studies, and in Church every Sunday. As time goes by the old behavior manifest itself and the recovering addict begins to feel as if they don't need as many meetings or they don't have to go to Bible studies and they can miss Church every once in a while. Slowly the old nature resurfaces, and they forget the main problem was not drugs and alcohol but the behavior and disobedience to God. This in turn leads to lying, cheating, and sexual misconduct. Once we get out of God's will, the thorn is released. The pain and suffering that caused this addiction returns, stronger than ever.

A person who is clean and sober and stops doing the things that got them there, will find out that just being clean and sober is not enough. The recovering person forgets where they came from; thinking that they have arrived or they have fully recovered and they are cured from this disease. So they stop working on themselves, they stop going to meeting and they stop studying their Word. Unbeknown to them they have turned their back on God once again, but because God loves for them, God has a way of getting their attention by allowing that monster (drugs and alcohol) to be released again.

Psychologists have found that 5% of a recovering person's problem is drugs and alcohol, and 95%--the person themselves. Pride, arrogance, selfishness, and sexual misconduct all cause a recovering addict to return to what he knows best and that's drinking and getting high.   When you get out of God's will, the only other will is Satan's will.   There is no in-between. Once you start participating in these old behaviors, the sleeping giant (addiction/alcoholism) is awakened and the only thing that can arrest that monster again is the power of God through repentance.

Unfortunately, some addicts/alcoholics have to hit another bottom before they surrender again. Never forget, every bottom has a trap door. The most cunning, powerful, yet baffling, component of this disease is its ability to convince a recovering person that he/she is okay or well.

Satan deceives hundreds and hundreds of recovering alcoholics/addicts into believing that they are well or normal. Therefore, they go out with the intention to take one drink, one hit or one fix. Forgetting the disease factor; that one drink, hit, or fix turns into two, three and so on. Their lives are like an out-of-control train racing downhill, they cannot stop, and once again, they find themselves on the bottom, using and abusing.

The disease of addiction is cunning. It will deceive a person and tell him he is doing fine. Then this person will stop working on himself. The disease is also baffling. It will confuse, bewilder, and frustrate the user and slowly steal the self-esteem and joy from his life. This disease is also powerful. It will consume, control and destroy everything and everyone that gets in its path.

The Bible says in II Peter 5: 8, *"The devil is like a roaring lion seeking whom he may devour."* Never underestimate the disease of addiction. Satan's job is to kill, steal, and destroy.   Many Christians have been deceived into thinking that they can go back to sociable drinking and using.   The disease of addiction is real and can be arrested only if they continue taking the right medicine.

For the Christian counselor entering into this field of addiction, he must be ready to discover the disobedience in every addict/alcoholic that asks for help. Our disobedience has allowed Satan to have his way with our lives. As long as we allow a little sin in, we will be subject to anything that Satan has to offer.

The roaring lion is looking for disobedient Christians, and once they are found, that lion will destroy them by any means necessary. We have to teach our people how to be "on guard;" watching and praying, and honestly examining themselves daily to see if they are being doers of the Word in all their affairs.

Recognizing your character flaws will be a very important part of your recovery, and for some this is a very large hurdle. Mind you, this is only the beginning. Just knowing you have these flaws does not fix the situation. Learning how to change those character defects will be the next hurdle. The key to winning each battle is knowing that you cannot fix yourself. It is going to take a power greater than you and that power is our Lord and Savior Jesus Christ. The all-important question is how do you get this power to work for you? First, accept Jesus Christ as your personal Lord and Savior, and second, you must live the Word of God.

John 8:32, "You shall know the truth and the truth shall make you free." The word **know** in this sentence is translated in the Greek as **"live."** It is the recognition of 'truth' through personal experience. Here, some type of action must take place. For example, once you know you have an attitude problem; it's not good enough to just "know" you have a problem; you have to work on changing the problem. There are three prescriptions that must be taken in order to win this battle against addiction: *righteousness, holiness and humility.* If you want God to put his stamp of approval on your life, live right for God (righteous). Holiness takes you into a special place in God where you set yourself apart for Him. Last, but certainly not least, is humility. This is very special in God's sight. The

Bible says to humble thyself before the Lord and He will lift you up. Humility is your main answer to pride, selfishness, and ego. These are the main defects of character that can bring an addict/alcoholic to their knees. This is living the Word of God and you are now well on your way to recovery. Asking God daily to help you change these behaviors will be your challenge. Remember, when there is "no" change there is "no" change. When there is no change, you stay the same, doing the same thing, and acting the same way. The definition of insanity is to "continue doing the same thing expecting different results."

1. Why is addiction and alcoholism considered a disease? (Give a full and complete answer.)

____

____

____

____

2. What are the two-standout flaws in most addicts/alcoholics? Explain how these flaws come alive in your life?

____

____

____

____

3. The causes of high blood pressure are the foods we eat, the stress of life, and lack of exercise. If addiction is a spiritual disease that centers in our mind, what are the causes?

____

____

4. When should a practicing addict/alcoholic seek help? What kept you from receiving help before you did?

____

____

____

5. Why did God allow Satan to afflict Paul with this affliction?

____

____

____

6. Now that we know what caused Paul's affliction, what should Paul have to do to work on that cause?

____

____

7. Why did God allow you to be afflicted with your disease? (There is more than one answer.)

____

____

____

8. What does "my grace is sufficient for you" mean?

____

____

9. What does II Peter 2:22 and relapse have in common with you?

____

____

10. If God never took the thorn out of Paul's side, how was Paul able to overcome his affliction?

____

____

11. How will you overcome your disease? (There is more than one answer.)

____

____

____

12. Explain the "invisible line" theory?

____

____

13. How did you get started drinking and (or) using drugs/alcohol?

____

____

____

14. Have you crossed that "fine invisible line"?   Yes ☐   No ☐

15. What was the incident that occurred in your life that made you realize you had crossed
that "fine invisible line"?

____

____

16. What does "hitting a bottom" mean? What was your bottom?

____

____

Remember at everybody's bottom, there is a trap door.

17. God forbid you fall through that trap door and return to drinking and using, but no one
knows you better than you. If you were to fall through that trap door again what would
be waiting for you on the other side of that trap door?

____

____

18. How can family members help the addict/alcoholic in "hitting their bottom"? (Explain
your answer fully.)

____

____

____

19. What three prescriptions are used to fight the battle that is raging inside the recovering
addict/alcoholic?

____

____

____

WHAT IS THE PROCESS OF RECOVERY &WHY?

Process is defined as: (1) a systematic series of actions directed to some end; (2) a continuous action, operation, or series of changes taking place in a definite manner. Recovery is defined as: (1) regaining something that is lost or taken away; (2) regaining strength, composure, and balance of oneself; (3) restoration or return to any former and better condition, especially to health from sickness, injury, addiction, etc.

(1) A systematic series of actions directed to some end; in this case it is a well thought out, organized plan with a beginning and an end. Most of the time this plan has already been tried, tested and proven to work by individuals that are free from addiction and still pressing towards Gods mark. In recovery, or even being a Christian you don't have to re-invent the wheel. Millions are free from drugs and alcohol and even more living a blessed Christian life style because they followed the footsteps of someone that went before them. (2) A continuous action, operation, or series of changes taking place in a definite manner. People that are successful in this recovery process have organizes lives. They organize their day down to the minute. From the moment they get up in the morning and falling on there knees in prayer with God to ending there day on their knees and everything in-between is planned. This carefully planned day looks nothing like the days before recovery. Many changes have to be adopted, and change will be their biggest hurtle. For some change is easy because daily they surrender to this new life.

Day in and day out sticking to that plan that worked for them in the beginning when they started recovery. Not only are you staying clean and sober but you are erasing bad habits and replacing them with new productive habits. One day these new habits turn into a new way of life, and at this point, you are well on your way to a better life. Where addicts and alcoholic tend to relapse is they think this is an overnight process. They think they can enter into a recovery program, stay in that program for six, nine, or 12 months and erase 2,5,15 years of bad habits, bad thinking, and bad behaviors. (3) Restoration or return to any former and better condition, especially to health from sickness, injury, addiction, etc. Many addicts or alcoholics long to return to any former condition before drinking and using, and for many, all they want is a return to life as they knew it before drinking and using. There are also those that came from dysfunctional families, and certainly, this is not what they want to go back too. Therefore, they begin a very new life in Christ, and the only example they see is those walking the same road they want to walk. Then you have those who can reach back into their life before drugs and alcohol and retrieve some of the morals and good behaviors that were taught to them as a kid.

The process of recovery was designed for addicts and alcoholics who have hit a spiritual, mental, and physical bottom. The process of recovery is not limited to just addicts and alcoholics. We have found that anyone who has lost his composure, or has fallen and cannot get up (as far as living is concerned) can benefit from this process.

The process of recovery is described as "the last house on the block" for many addicts/alcoholics. Most addicts have tried everything conceivable to quit drinking or using. Many attempt to reduce the drug and alcohol usage or switching to what they consider a lesser drug or drink. Some give their paychecks to their loved ones to hold so that love one can dispense it appropriately. Some go into programs to dry out hoping that by being removed from the environment, maybe, they will hear something that will keep them free. Some run to church (the building) thinking that this will fix them. However, without a serious relationship with God, many run back and forth, in and out of the Church, never experiencing true freedom and never achieving sobriety.

Some addicts try psychiatry, hypnosis, medically prescribed drugs, and even acupuncture to rid themselves of their addiction. For some this may work, but the majority returns to their personal bondage.

Addicts and alcoholics have been known to make geographical moves, going from state to state, city to city, neighborhood to neighborhood, always finding themselves in another city or state doing the same thing. One writer wrote, "Everywhere you go there you are." No matter what you do, you can't hide from yourself.

Some have even gone so far as to be willingly incarcerated, hoping this problem will go away. This doesn't work because the disease of addiction centers in the mind. As long as you can remember, the disease will be with you. This type of logic never works because as soon as the person is released from prison and returns to old or new neighborhood; he/she is bound to run into "triggers" and the mind will revert back to what it use to do and the person reacts the way they did in the past. Another reason going to jail is not a good idea is that there are drugs in jail.

The final act of separation from this disease is suicide. The pain becomes so great some people would rather die than live the way they have been living. For most addicts and alcoholics the fun of using and drinking left a long time ago. Most continue this lifestyle because they have to, not because they want to. They see no way out. Tunnel vision has set in and the end of the tunnel is nowhere in sight. When they look into their future, there is only darkness, hopelessness and despair.

During this process, God can meet you wherever you are and guide you back to a safe place in Christ Jesus. Existing on skid row, from vacant cars to abandon building, God can meet you there. If your skid row is in a fully furnished home that has turned into a prison, God will meet you there. Step by step, precept-by-precept, the process will teach you how to live a successful life in Him. Simple things that we take for granted will be offered to you in this process. These simple principles will bring order back into the lives of those addicted.

The 12 Spiritual Steps to recovery are arranged in a specific order for a reason. The first three steps of recovery introduce you to God.   Without God, we lean to our own understanding, and it was our own understanding that put us in the position we are in. We must never forget that we were doing our best thinking and we still became addicts or alcoholics. So put no trust in your own logic. Recovery is about renewing the mind, and be willing to change.

In recovery we share with others who are just like us, recovering people who are doing all they can to change and apply this process in their lives, sharing how they made it through difficult situations without drinking or using. The big book of Alcoholics Anonymous says one alcoholic helping another is therapeutic. Remember, God works through people. Don't be afraid to share your feelings, decisions, your ups and downs, and victories with other people. Once you surrender your life over to God, he orders your footsteps and will put people in your life that will be a blessing to you.

The next four steps introduce you to you.   From the time you took your very first drink, you altered your course in life, and the path that God had set for you. The more you drank and used, the further away you became. Once you became an addict/alcoholic you also became a fake, phony and fraud. Most addicts/alcoholics have a very small glimpse of "who" they really are, and others are not sure about that. If we ask them "will the real *(put their name here)* please stand up, many would have a hard time standing. When living that lifestyle they become whatever it took to continue drinking and using. Drifting farther away from the person God would have them to be.

The next two steps help you to understand your relationship with people who are close to you. Your loved ones, your family members, and your close friends have all been affected by your behavior. Many bridges have been destroyed because of your drinking and using, and at this stage of recovery, honesty once again is key. They ask a question in the program, "What part did you have to play in it?" What part did you have to play in a failed relationship? God is able to fix any bridge that has been destroyed, if you trust in Him, apply this process in your life, and allow this mighty move of faith to work for you.

The last three steps are called maintenance steps. As you live your life one day at a time, these steps help you keep focused on your recovery and on your growth in God.

Here, no one can do the work for you. You have to do it for yourself. Be not afraid, God will never leave you or forsake you.   The process of recovery works, but it takes work on your part.

Today as Bible believing Christians, we can't afford to be afraid to ask God why we are losing this war against drugs and alcohol. So we ask, "If Jesus is everything that we believe He is, why are we losing this war against drug and alcohol addiction? Could it be we, as the Church, are doing something wrong? Maybe most people believe this is a self-inflicted disease and God is allowing people to suffer because they brought this upon themselves?

All through the Word of God, God the Father restored hurting people, and today is no different. We who enter into God's presence, broken into many pieces, worked hard at trying to fix ourselves, but it did not happen. Only an all-powerful God can complete this reconstruction of heart, mind, soul and spirit. Nevertheless, we have to be willing to go through this process in order to gain complete recovery. Many addicts and alcoholics have been delivered from their addiction by walking into a Church, having anointed laid hands on them, and becoming freed by God that day. However, at the same time, many walk into that same Church, and the same hands were laid on them and these addicts continued to use. Yes, God can complete the job with one touch, but for reasons only known by God we see God moving in a different direction. This direction is called the Process of Recovery. In this process, we see God, in His all-powerful wisdom, making the addict/alcoholic get involved in his own healing process.   God has given us instructions on how an addict/alcoholic should start this process called recovery.

Romans 12:2 says, *"And do not be conformed to this world but be **transformed by the renewing of your mind**, that you may prove what is that good and acceptable and perfect will of God."* In order for this miraculous change to take place we must take one step and God will take two.

Those starting this road to recovery must examine their worldly activities and be willing to eliminate these activities from their lives. Those who want to continue holding on to these worldly ways will find themselves riding on a dangerous merry-go-round where nothing is "merry" anymore.

SO WHY THE PROCESS OF RECOVERY?

We believe that this process called Recovery is God's ram in the bush or God's plan "B" which is as good as plan "A," the laying on of hands. We have seen God work miracles in the lives of practicing alcoholics/addicts all over the world. Before the process of recovery, the Church witnessed God's power through the laying on of hands, with one touch, healing takes place. With one touch, the power of the Holy Spirit has set some people free faster than you can blink an eye. Still questions arise and have to be confronted; What about the addict or alcoholic who walks into that same Church, on that same day, gets hands laid on them by the same man of God, and yet return to drinking and using? What is wrong with them? Or does the Church have an answer that will rescue them?

Yes, God has an answer for them. Yes, there is a ram in the bush. We believe this ram in the bush is called the "Process of Recovery." We who have been freed through this process called recovery thank God for it.

What is good about the process of recovery is it kills several birds with one stone. The process clearly lets you confront one situation while working on another. The process allows you to come to God with a drug or alcohol addiction. Then God will allow one to confront their prideful behavior which brought the drug and alcohol addiction on in the beginning, thus, killing two birds with one stone.

The process helps you to get honest with yourself and in turn shows you who you really are in Christ. It also teaches you how to surrender to God daily, knowing that God has all power. It reminds you that you are not in control of your life. The process teaches you that there is a power greater than yourself. Then it will introduce you to "the" power, Christ Jesus our Lord and Savior, who has all power.

Once you have developed a personal relationship with God, He will show you, with the help of a counselor or sponsor, some of those bad habits you picked up while you were separated from Him. Once you learn how to recognize these defects of character, the process teaches you how to walk through situations in a Christ-like manner, and thus you grow. As you travel through each step, the process will open doors that most people avoid while in their addiction. The process of recovery will help us to identify and face our feelings, good or bad, when we go through the challenges of life without drinking or using.

1. Define recovery?

____

____

____

2. List the people, places and things that must be eliminated from your life to start this road to recovery.

____

____

____

3. What are you attempting to recover, what is it you want restored? (List and explain why.)

____

____

____

4. Has any clergy ever "laid hands" on you concerning your drug and alcohol addiction? Yes ☐   No ☐

5. What happened?

____

____

6. Define process? (As it applies to recovery.)

____

____

7. How did you attempt to quit drinking and using before you were introduced to the process of recovery? (List and explain.)

____

____

8. Why is the process of recovery important?

____

____

9. Why is the process of recovery considered the "last house on the block?"

____

____

10. In this "process called recovery", what behavior will you be looking to eliminate?

____

____

11. The process of recovery meets the practicing addict/alcoholic where they are, and leads that person in the direction God would have for them to go. Where is God leading you?

____

____

____

THERE IS POWER IN BEING POWERLESS

If there was ever a concept in the Bible or in the field of recovery that logically makes no sense at all, this has got to be it. "There is power in being powerless". Receiving power after willingly becoming powerless is the concept. *(1Peter 5:6, Humble yourselves under the mighty hand of God, that He may exalt you in due time.)* Humbling yourself, denying yourself, receiving no glories, claiming no power of your own, and in return, God vesting you with all power. As I said, it makes no sense.

Here we must accept Jesus Christ as our personal Lord and Savior to understand this important concept. You must have a "spiritual third eye" to "see" this powerful insight.

The world, the unsaved, has a hard time understanding this Godly law. Powerlessness is one of the greatest weapons used in this battle with sinful behavior. It is used to keep a person from practicing an out of control behavior. To the world, 2 + 2 has to equal four. Willingly becoming powerless and God giving you all power in return, does not compute.

Those that believe they have power struggle in life when people, places, things, or situations do not go the way they think they should go. In many circles, this can be defined as control. Controlling people want people to act the way they want them to act. They want people to do what they want them to do, and when they don't it is hard for them to let them be ok with their decision. They get irritated, frustrated, annoyed, and even angered because things that are out of their control don't go as they have planned.

Controlling behaviors can also be very destructive. What happens when two people come together that are in denial about their "control" issues. Who gives in? What happens when neither person submits? Animosity, resentment, bitterness can destroy a relationship and like an infectious disease it can spread throughout a family/friend structure, and or office environment etc. People will be force to choose sides because no one recognizes this sinful sickness called "Control" that is fueling the situation.

Powerlessness is one of the greatest weapons used in this battle against this sinful behavior. When people offend us, come into our space, disagree with us; powerlessness teaches us to let them be who they are. A person who thinks he has power enters into relapse mode trying to control, direct, or influence other people's thoughts, deeds or actions. A person who is trying their best to have peace in their lives can easily be distracted trying to control situations that they have no power over. Finally, frustration gets the best of them; they return to their old thinking and react the way they used to act, slowly returning them back to drama, disease, or pain in their lives.

For many, applying "powerless" to your life is easier said than done, especially when "school or the streets" has taught us to be powerful. The world that we live in today teaches us to attack every threatening situation head on, confronting these situations when they arise. The only problem is, when we do this we end up leaving no room for God to work in our lives. Many of us take our problems to the altar and we leave that altar with those same problems in our hands, never turning them over to God. God's desire is to help us with our problems but we get in the way! Knowing when to surrender and letting God move on your behalf will be your quest. The Bible tells us at Psalm 46:10 *"be still and know that I am God."* For someone that has been in control of their life for most of their lives struggle in this area. People who are prone to control, direct, or fix situations never leave room for God to perform a miracle. They are so used to attacking every situation they end up in God's way. People like this have to learn how to pray and wait for an answer.

In your attempt to rid yourself of this sinful behavior, you have to admit that you cannot stop on your own. (You are powerless.) Next, it will take a power greater than yourself (Jesus) to relieve you of the pain and suffering that you've experienced. Here the individual recognizes that he or she has no power to stop. "Powerless"

Paul explains it best in Romans 7:15 (New Living Translation) *"I don't understand myself at all, for I really want to do what is right, but I don't do it. Instead, I do the very thing I hate. (16) I know perfectly well what I am doing is wrong, and my bad conscience shows that I agree the law is good. (17) But I can't help myself, because it is the sin inside me that makes me do these evil things."* Here Paul explains that he is trying to stop doing whatever it was he was doing, but he can't stop. Understand this is a man who was starting Churches everywhere he went. He also wrote thirteen (13) books of the Bible. This is no ordinary man. This man knew the Lord well, and was a diligent worker for the Lord. However, there was something that he was doing. Paul describes it as a practice, and he surely could not stop on his own power. At verse 24 Paul says, *"O wretched man that I am. Who will deliver me from this body of death?"* Paul is looking for help and it comes in the very next verse (25) Paul says, *"I thank God through Jesus Christ our Lord."* Once the individual stop fighting this disorder with their own power, and surrenders, God steps in and fights the battle for them.

Powerlessness moves a person into an area that is loved by God. This area is a gift to some and others have to work hard to obtain it. Once you 'taste' and experience this area you automatically know that you have experienced a quality that is honored by God. It is honored by God because you are now taking steps to Trust God. (This is a new area for controlling people) Powerlessness is defined as humility in the Word of God. Humility is the direct opposite of everything that Satan stands for. A prideful and arrogant behavior is the reason Satan was kicked out of heaven. Today we see that the biggest problem an individual that is practicing this sinful behavior is his or her pride. Humbling yourself means denying yourself, receiving no glories, claiming no power of your own and receiving all power through Jesus Christ.

Once you start practicing powerlessness in your life, you enter into the presence of almighty God. Here you are able to see God work miracles in your life; and the only possible explanation is that it was God that healed, fixed or changed, these situations. How can God get the glory if you still think you can fix the crisis you are in? As soon as you think you can fix it, God has left the situation. God will not get in the way of the power you think you have!

Powerlessness can also be defined as surrendering. Letting go and letting God! Letting God do for you in every situation because you surrendered your will to Him and trust Him. Proverb 3:5-6 tells us, *"Trust in the Lord with all thine heart and lean not unto thane own understanding, in all thy ways acknowledge Him and He will direct thy path."*

Countless times addicts/alcoholics get into trouble, and repeatedly they call on God for help. Praise God, for His Word says, *"I will never leave you or forsake you."* God is always there to help them out of their predicament. Once God comes to the rescue and the fog has lifted, and the recovering person can see again, some addicts can't wait to return to some of, or all, of their old behaviors. They return to fixing situations without looking to God. So, the question has to be asked…are you ready to be a full-time Christian? Are you ready to turn your will and life over to the will of God, one day at a time? Or, are you just keeping God close for times of need? How do you think God feels when His own people use him like a spiritual Santa Claus; only calling Him when they want something?

How do you become powerless? How do you totally surrender to God? First, let us look at some definitions:

First, humble yourself. Learning how to be modest, meek in spirit, and unassuming in all your affairs will be the challenge of a lifetime. Turn the other cheek, avoid drama, and sometimes even when you are right and you know you are right, you give in to keep the peace. Give up your right to be right. Now, this does not mean you let people run over you. This means you learn how to avoid unchangeable situation. Once you learn how to become powerless over people, you allow them to be who they are and not let them affect you and your recovery.   LET GO AND LET GOD!

Second, <u>deny yourself and put the needs of others before your own</u>. Here you begin to develop a caring spirit. When practicing powerlessness, we do not have to be first any more, or be the best. The world teaches us that life is a sprint and the one with the most toys at the end wins. This is totally opposite to what the Word of God teaches us. Put another person's needs before yours and God will take care of you. This takes the pressure off us, and we can watch God work miracles in our lives as we help others. Do not get me wrong, we keep "pressing towards the mark of the high calling in Christ Jesus," but now that we are practicing powerlessness our mark has changed. Today we are seeking first the kingdom of God. Our goal is not to be first or the best, our goal is to serve God's people, and if God sees fit to elevate us to the first or the best, wherever, so be it.

Third, receive no glory. "Don't believe the hype." Once God pulls you out of the hell that you were once in, after God picks you up and turns you around, once God begins to bless you financially, and opens doors that were once closed to you, remember to give God all the glory.   People will pat you on the back and tell you what a great job you are doing— "don't believe the hype." You will take a look at your possessions, houses, cars, and money in the bank—"don't believe the hype." Promotions on jobs, successful ministries— "don't believe the hype." All that you are is because Jesus died on the cross for your sins. Because we love, trust, and believe in Him, God has blessed us because we are obedient to His will.

Understanding powerlessness also allows us to enter into acceptance.   Acceptance gives us peace in the middle of the storm. Here we understand that wherever we are, we are right where God wants us to be, never forgetting God is in control. The Word of God tells us that every Christian will be faced with trials and tribulations. Just because we accepted Christ into our lives does not mean that we go through life without any problems. I Corinthians 10:13 let's us know that, *"No temptation has overtaken you that is not common to man, God is faithful, and he will not let you be tempted beyond your strength, but with the temptation will also provide the way of escape, that you may be able to endure it."* We in recovery have to accept what life brings, knowing that God is with us and will be there for us. How does a recovering person go through a storm without drinking or using? Using the tools that you learn in the process of recovery is the beginning. Not going through life's ups and down alone is very important to the person going through difficult times. Along with praying, fasting, and going through your trials one day at a time we recognize that God is with us and He knows what we are going through.

In Daniel 3:19-30, the three Hebrew boys Shadrach, Meshach, and Abed-Nego, were faced with a no win situation in the eyes of the world. King Nebuchadnezzar threatened to throw them into the fire if they did not bow down and worship his god. ***Powerless*** over this situation they ***accepted*** the decision that the king handed down, and without worrying, arguing, or fighting they went into the fire. Because they ***accepted*** their fate and did not bow down because of the King's threats, God saw them through a horrible situation.

Today we are faced with our own personal trials. Trials that we have no control over; God shows all power in powerless situations. After the three Hebrew boys were thrown into the fire and the furnace was turned to its highest degree, the Bible says, "*King Nebuchadnezzar was astonished; and he rose and spoke, saying to his counselors, "Did we not cast three men bound into the midst of the fire?" They answered and said to the king, "True, O king." "Look" he answered, "I see four men loose, walking in the midst of the fire: and they are not hurt, and the form of the fourth is like the Son of God".* Today for an example, the boss tells an employee there is going to be a layoff or downsizing in their place of employment. Using ***power,*** this employee will do everything in his/her power to stop this layoff from happening, or they will worry until they take a drink, or has a fix, or makes themselves sick. ***Acceptance*** teaches we accept the bad news believing God for a better job. ***Acceptance,*** faith and powerlessness go hand in hand.

The day we start thinking we have power, over people places, or things, God has left the situation. For recovering people that "play god," sooner or later, they are headed for another fall. Drinking and using because nothing is going the way *they* planned it, and once again God has to come to the rescue pulling us out of that horrible pit. Because of God's love for us, He is willing to let us go; and once we fall, He is there to pick us up and give us another chance.

We as recovering people that have accepted Christ into our lives, have to make up our minds on what we really want to do concerning our lives. Do we really want to be Christians, living righteous and holy, doing the work that God has called us to do; or do we want to return to that old lifestyle, with or without, the drugs or alcohol? Alternatively, do we want to meet somewhere in the middle, one foot in the world and the other in Christ? Those who constantly relapse have a hard time answering these questions honestly.

It's very easy for the addict/alcoholic to tell the counselor, loved ones or friends what they want to hear: but, to search themselves and put forth the effort to follow God, they rather not do it. Here are just some of the reasons they struggle:

- Some never trust God to do what He said He could do.
- Some are not ready to be full time 24 hour, 7 days a week Christians.
- Some have not made up their minds on what they want to do altogether, so they continue wandering through life year in and year out totally lost, never finding freedom. They go in and out of programs and jails or institutions never accomplishing anything in life.
- Some die in their disease because they never make up their mind to surrender or they choose to do their own thing without God.

Once again, God allows us to make the decision to be powerless. The only good thing about being on the bottom is once you are there; all you can do is look up.

Once you tap into this powerful gift called powerlessness, your outlook on life will change. You will find the power that you have today is God's power working on your behalf. Don't get it twisted! Learn to sit back and relax "Let Go and Let God." There is power in being powerless.

1. Why is "powerless" so important to the recovering alcoholic addict? (Explain fully.)

____

____

____

2. What does "denying one's self" mean?

____

____

3. The definition of pride is arrogance, conceit, smugness, and self-importance. List the behaviors that you notice in yourself and explain.

____

____

____

4. What is the danger in receiving glory or believing you have power?

____

____

____

5. At the end of chapter the writer writes, "The only good thing about being on the bottom is, once you are there, all you can do is look up." If you are looking up in your life, what do you see? (List and explain why.)

____

____

____

6. In your own words, how would you see yourself as a full-time Christian, even though you may not be there now?

____

____

____

7. List the things recovering people have to do to stay clean & sober.

____

____

____

8. Do you think you are controlling? Yes   No

9. Has anyone ever called you "controlling" or "control freak", nosey, or busy-body?

Yes No

10. If yes, are you willing to change? Yes No

THE RECOVERING ALCOHOLIC/ADDICT

The day a we decide to surrender and get help through the process, it is this day that we become a recovering person. If we give ourselves a chance, we will find many different tools to stay clean and sober.

Here, the recovering alcoholic/addict has to learn how to live a Christ-centered lifestyle to stay free. Going to and participating in meetings will be a part of this process of recovery; fellowshipping with saints, and getting a sponsor will be another part of the process.

Fellowshipping is just another way of saying "spending time with" or "hanging out with" people that you admire and because of how they live you want what they have. These recovering people carry themselves in a way that is pleasing to the recovering addict/alcoholic.

A sponsor is someone who has been clean at least a year of any mind-altering substance (see "Why a Sponsor" in Chapter II). The Sponsor has to be familiar with the 12 Steps and the Process of Recovery. A sponsor will take the new comer and walk with them through this process. The new comer periodically reports to the sponsor to make sure he/she is on the right track.

The new comer now entering this new journey is at a very delicate point in their life. This is especially true for those who get involved in the Church. Recovering people are taught early in the process that their addiction is a disease, and that while this disease rarely, or never goes away, it can be arrested. When a recovering addict/alcoholic surrenders to this fact and recognizes that God has released him from this bondage of hell that he was in, a special bond is created between Jesus and the addict/alcoholic who had been doomed for death.

We in recovery know that what Satan meant for destruction, God can use to his glory. Once an addict recognizes that he or she cannot control their addiction, they are ready to begin their road to recovery. A person who totally surrenders listens as only the dying can. This person is ready for recovery when they recognize, and fully understand that no human power can save them. Here the recovering person has to work on the total man. Each person has a three-fold nature: mind, body, spirit. **All three have to be healed.**

I) The Mind --
    A) Is effected by our warped thinking.
        1) Music sounds better when I am high.
        2) I can talk to the opposite sex better when I am high.
        3) These are my friends and I can't leave them.
    B) Will rationalize our condition and why we do what we do.
        1) God made the weed, or coca plant, so it's okay.
        2) It's my life and I am not hurting anyone but myself.
    C) Is controlled by the drug. Certain things will trigger the craving.
        1) The opposite sex.
        2) Money
        3) Hanging out in dangerous places, bars, clubs, etc.

II) The Body --
  A) The craving is unbearable and the body will shut down if not satisfied.
      1) Heroin and alcohol are just a two drugs that will send the body into withdrawals if not properly regulated when coming off some drugs.
      2) The mental craving of crack cocaine will make the strongest of men surrender their lives over to this all-powerful drug. Causing most to go without eating, sleeping, and disregarding medically prescribed prescriptions that are needed to survive, thus tearing the body down.
      3) The wear and tear on the body is sometimes irreversible, leading to sickness or even death.
III) The Spirit
  A) The lifeline of the individual.
  B) The lack of spiritual connection. (Cuts his/herself off from God.)
  C) Loses all moral values. (Does not care about anything.)
      In order for a recovering person to live a drug and alcohol free lifestyle, we must first:
      1) Learn how to take suggestions. - Walking in recovery is something new to the addict/alcoholic. There are many people who have walked this path ahead of you; so, learn how to listen, and become teachable.
      2) Be disciplined. - We must have his/her priorities in order and stick to them, no matter what.
      3) Be willing to change. - When there is no change, there is no change. We must be willing to change (not people, places, and things).
      4) Not be willing to get well, but to get better. - Always pressing towards the mark of the high calling in Christ Jesus. Never act as if you have arrived.

We who are successful in staying free have two things in common when we began this journey called recovery. One, we *"listen like only the dying can"*. Two, we cried out to God as if death was the only thing left. We take recovery seriously and will not let anything get in their way.

We are willing to change, and we do that by taking suggestions. We understand that this change will not take place quickly and this is not an overnight process. Once again, one day at a time they have to examine their every step for appropriate change to take place.

In the beginning, recognizing our faults and abnormal behaviors is the first hurtle. We have to be honest enough to identify your faults. No one comes into recovery without character defects. So, we have to be willing to take an honest look at our self or be willing to except honest criticism.

Being open and honest with another human being and sharing our deepest darkest secrets are what we do to free ourselves from our past. This is a very important part of the healing process. The Bible tells us in James 5:16 *to "Confess thy faults one to another and pray one for another that you may be healed."* One person said, "Confession is good for the soul."   In the groups of recovery, they have a saying "you are as sick as your secrets." Last, but certainly not least, and this may be the highest hurdle, you now have to change those faults you have identified. Come up with a plan and be willing to execute that plan at a moments notice. We can't afford to handle difficult situations the way we used to. When there is no change – there is no change.

We picked up many bad habits while we were out there using and abusing our bodies, and it is a wonder that we are still sane. Our bodies, our minds and our spirits are all affected because of practicing abnormal behavior.

Can you teach old dog new tricks? Of course you can. With the power of the Holy Ghost, good teaching, and a willing heart all things are possible.

Remember staying free won't take much, but it will take all you've got.

1. How is the mind affected? (Use your own words.)

____

____

2. How is the body affected? (Use your own words.)

____

____

3. How is the spirit affected? (Use your own words.)

____

____

4. Making a change from a cocoon to a butterfly is not an easy thing to do. What will be your biggest change other than drugs or alcohol? Attitude? Lifestyle? Associates? All of the above? (List and explain.)

____

____

____

____

5. How far are you willing to go to stay free from your addiction?

____

____

6. List two (2) of your faults. What are the motives behind these faults, why are they a part of your life?

____

____

____

7.   Why does confessing your faults heal you?

____

____

____

UNDERSTANDING RELAPSE

Before I get started, I want to destroy a myth that seems to be floating around the rooms of recovery. This rumor is: relapse is a part of your recovery. For some strange reason some people believe that in order to fully participate and receive all that the process of recovery offers, you have to go in and out of treatment until you really make up your mind to quit. It's almost as if they're looking for a "good enough bottom" to get serious. A "good enough bottom" means now you are doing some of those things that you said you never do and you have to destroy those relationships around you and hurt your love ones and burn all your bridges. A "good enough bottom" meaning they are looking for that one thing that will make them say, "enough is enough," unfortunately some never find it.

Those that enter into recovery believing "another bottom" will be the motivating factor that will turn their life around will continue to relapse. Remember, "Everybody's bottom has a trap door," you can fall even lower than where you have fallen. Do you really want to know what's on the other side of your trap door? So you have to ask yourself what could be worse than this bottom you're on? For some its jails, institutions, or even death! A "good enough bottom" does not mean you have to lose everything or find out what's on the other side of that trap door. All it takes is being tired of what's been going on in your life and a surrender spirit. The idea that you have to hit a horrible bottom is one way to get started, but it is not the only way. Some are introduced to recovery, they hear your story, and that's enough!

Once we hear the good news of Jesus Christ, we never have to take another drink, fix, or hit again as long as you live.

We know that some people do relapse, and we thank God that there is a safe place to come and begin this process over again. However, it is not necessary to continue to fall. Today can be your last day of drinking and using. Once you read this, you do not have to practice your disease any more if you don't want to in Jesus' name.

We know for a fact that those who follow our path to freedom can claim freedom one day at a time. It is surely our goal that one day men and women will grab hold to this freedom that God is willing to give to all of us. All it takes is a made-up mind, a surrendered heart, and be willing to take some suggestions. Freedom is yours for the taking. The greatest gift ever given to anyone is the gift of life. Just by accepting Jesus Christ as your personal Lord and Savior, we live with Jesus forever. It's that simple. If living with the Lord forever were so easy, why would Jesus make freedom hard to come by?

For those who relapse, our love for you is just as strong. We understand the disease of addiction is cunning, baffling and powerful. However, we also know a God that has never lost a battle.

If you relapse, we beg you to get back up and try again. It is God's desire that every man be free. As long as you have breath in your body, you have a chance to tap into this freedom. We that work in the field of recovery pray that no one ever returns to using and abusing drugs or alcohol, but we know that relapse happens. There are mainly two types of "recovering people" that relapse.

1. There is the person that never sought recovery, but knew they had a problem so they decided to stop on their own. Most of them last until the next paycheck, and the desire becomes too great so they return to the drug or drink of their choice. This group has a slim chance being free from their addiction. Their lack of knowledge concerning their illness leaves them with little or no chance to stay completely free.
2. This person seeks some type of professional help. They either enter into a drug/alcohol in-house or outpatient program. Alternatively, they will attend support group meetings (AA, NA, CA, Free N One meetings). This person fails to submit to the tools that were given to them, so they return to the bondage they once were in. This group never believes this disease concept or they try the information that has been given to them, believing that it can't get that bad again.

Anyone that starts recovery has to be aware of relapse and what can cause it. One of the first things you have to be aware of is triggers. A trigger can be thoughts of anything that brings back thoughts, feelings, and memories that have to do with addiction. A persons surrounding environment are filled with triggers, be it visual, something you see on T.V. or riding through and old neighborhood or seeing an old friend. Triggers could be jarred by something you hear, a song, some ones voice over the telephone. It could be a smell, someone smoking a cigarette can remind the brain of pleasures associated with addiction. Triggers can happen as quickly as a light switch turning on and the craving can overpower a person within minutes.

The process of recovery first helps the addict/alcoholic to recognize the triggers that can cause the craving. Next the process gives you tools to overcome them.

There are signs to relapse that happen way before a person drinks or uses. People in the rooms of recovery call it pre-lapse. You really don't have to be a therapist or someone that's been in the rooms of recovery to recognize the symptoms. But you must understand the *Disease of Addiction* to know what to look for.

People that show symptoms of catching a cold may start off with a scratchy throat, running nose, stuffy head, or congestion we automatically go into defensive mold and attack these symptoms with over the counter medicine or home remedies or both.

Well the same watchful eye is needed in recovery. The *Disease of Addiction* is liken to a cold and before a person takes a drink or a hit there is a change in their behavior. Some call it the "Dry Drunk syndrome. This term refers to someone who is not drinking or using yet, but they have already relapsed emotionally. They become restless, irritable, and discontent.

Everyone experience these feeling in the course of their recovery. The key to overcoming these feelings is having people around you that can see that something is different in your behavior and you are willing to examine yourself and take some suggestion.

- Restless – agitated, impatient, on edge, frantic, a feeling of disconnect.

- Irritable - short-tempered, touchy, sensitive, picky, cranky

- Discontent – unhappy, displeasure, dissatisfaction

When these three symptoms show up in our life, relapse is not that far away. The disease is untreated and they usually return to drinking or using. Others just become bitter and chase people away from them.

For those on the outside looking in are confused as they watch their love ones surrender to God, or surrender to the recovery process, do well for a while and return back to drinking and using. They don't understand how a person could put their hands in God's hands and one day snatch their hands away, and return to drinking and using. Until you understand the disease of addiction you will be baffled by this behavior.

Why do they continue to destroy their lives? Many family members, love-one and friends are asking this question as we speak. Why do they seem to fall in love with this new life in Christ and one day turn back to a life of destruction?

The *Process of Recovery* is medicine for the recovering person. Like cough medicine for a person that has a cold, the *Process of Recovery* is medicine for the recovering person. If they don't take their medicine they will cough.

We that work in this field of recovery know that there is no one specific answer. To blame it on the devil may be true, but addicts, alcoholic and their family members need more. They want to know the actual trick Satan uses to deceive the one they love.

One thing we witness in those that come out of an addiction and those that relapse is the overwhelming need to satisfy the flesh. They never grasp how frail the flesh is after it has been in bondage for longs periods of time. Many grow accustom to the bondage. It has been such a big part of their lives that drinking and using seems normal and not drinking and using seems foreign. *Harriet Tubman said, "I freed a thousand slaves I could have freed a thousand more if only they knew they were slaves."* When Harriet Tubman showed up on plantations to free the slaves many said "No"! They had accepted this lifestyle as normal and continued working for the slave owner. The Bible definition of Recovery is *"renewing the mind."* The disease of addiction centers in the mind and as long as a person can remember they are at risk to relapse.

Addicts and alcoholic with an untreated disease move through life hoping the old life will never return. However, the bible says at *Mark: 14:38 Watch and pray so that you will not fall into temptation. The spirit is willing but the flesh is weak.* Those that enter into this new life in Christ never realize how vulnerable they really are. This is why we recognize the disease concept and "watch and pray" with tools that will help them stay clean and sober. (See the Disease of Addiction) Those that enter into this new life in Christ try to convince themselves that the problem is gone never to return. But we know that (and here is where the disease comes in) as long as you can <u>remember </u>the threat to drink and use is there.

Another thing we see in the "relapse of an individual" there is lack of faith in the area of patience. *The bible says at Psalm 27:14 Wait for the Lord; be strong and take heart and wait for the Lord.* They want things to happen right now! They tend to forget that they have destroyed everything in their path, and what took years to build, years to establish, they want God to restore right now! They want their family members to trust them right now! "Don't you see me going to church; don't you see me making my meetings; why won't you trust me"? They want that good job right now! They want God to give them everything back in their time. They forget that God is in control of their lives and He will work it out when He wants too and how He wants too. Impatience they move without God, once again doing there own thing. They snatch their hands right out of God's hand leaving them unprotected, and before they know it, they roam around aimlessly like lost sheep and they are led astray. The bible says in *Hebrews 6:12 We do not want you to become lazy, but to imitate those who through faith and patience inherit what has been promised.* Learning how to endure without complaining trusting in God will be vital to the recovering persons well being. Complaining only puts a person is in a frustrated state of mind which allows them to focus on the problem instead of God the solution. Your time is not God's time and it is best to learn *how to be still and know that He is God* and has your best interest at heart.

Those that relapse, find out that not only is it bad, but most of the time it's worse. No matter how much clean and sober time they have accumulated, once they return to drinking and using, it's as if they had never left and the pain and suffering is just as bad. Luke 11:24-26 *says, "When an unclean spirit goes out of a man he goes through dry places, seeking rest; and finding none, he says I will return to my house from which I came (25) And when he comes, he finds it swept and put in order. (26) Then he goes and takes with him seven other spirits more wicked than himself, and they enter and dwell there and the last state of that man is worse than the first."* Here the word of God tells us that once we clean our house, *and* put it in order, if we don't fill it with God's presence, the demon that lived there at one time will return with seven of its friends. And they will make your life worse than it was in the beginning.

Applying this process to your life, there are some things that you should be aware of falling into relapse mode.

1. <u>Frustration</u> – is a common emotional response to opposition. Because, today, we no longer run and hide from frustrating situations we turn to our Free N One meetings, or sponsors. Learning how to share about frustrating situation is important when staying clean and sober. Here we talk about the feelings that come with everyday life. We have to be careful that we do not allow circumstances to aggravate, upset, discourage, or irritate us. When sharing with new clean and sober friends we find out that we are not the only ones that have traveled down this path. The Bible teaches us that we have sometimes encourage ourselves. *I Samuel 30:6 says, "Now David was greatly distressed for the people spoke of stoning him because the soul of all the people was grieved, every man for his sons and daughters."* But David ***encouraged himself in the Lord his God.***

2. <u>Boldness or Cockiness</u> -When we start thinking we are normal, or well, or we have arrived at a place in our lives where we don't need the fellowship, we don't need meetings, we don't need God's principals be careful lest you fall. When you don't fear the drugs or alcohol any longer, we are on the road to relapse. When we walk around patting ourselves on the back instead of giving God the Glory, we separate ourselves from God covering, and in God's love for us He will allow Satan to attack to get your attention again. Those that relapse forget it was God that rescued them from the horrible pit, and they move about life as if we were never addicts/alcoholics. When we forget where we came from and the pain that brought us into recovery, we are setting ourselves up for a big fall.

3. <u>Depression</u> - Allowing situations (that most of the times are out of our control) bring us down. We start seeing that we are down more times than we are up. Call your sponsor, make a meeting and share about what is going on with you. What you will find out that you are not alone, and many have been down the same road. If

you don't release the pressure that is building up inside of you, like a pressure cooker it will blow its top. We blow our tops at the liquor store or dope house.

4. <u>Impatience</u> -Wanting things to happen right now. Everything and everybody has to line up to what you want and do what you want them to do, when you want them to do it. When people don't line up the way you want and they rebel you become frustrated. Ongoing frustration leads you down a dangerous road.

5. <u>Selfishness</u> – Putting our needs before everyone else is a sure separation from God. Recovering people that separate themselves from their families and stop caring about those around them usually end up in relapse mode. The word Christian means to be Christ–like. Jesus always put people before himself, even unto the cross.

6. <u>Self-Pity</u> - Because of life's difficulties, recovering people tend to only focus on their own problems. We carry our troubles around everywhere we go, always searching for someone that will feel sorry for us. So they complain constantly about their situation and where they are in life. People that love playing the victim fall into this category.

7. <u>Ungrateful</u> - Forgetting where God has brought you from and taking for granted the people that helped you get where you are today. This person thinks he has something to do with his recovery. They never focus on how far they've come only the new life and its struggles.

8. <u>Exhaustion</u> – (a) Trying to catch up with lost time, by becoming a workaholic. (b) Working through the process of recovery as fast as you can. (c) Believing you owe the people around you, so you volunteer for every project that comes your way. Allowing love ones to make you feel guilty for your past wrongs, especially your kids. You will work hard at making up to them and they can make you feel like you can't do enough. Apologize and move on.

9. <u>Disobedience</u> – The biggest problem for all addicts and alcoholics. From the beginning they do what they want to do. Not caring about the law, their loved ones or any vow they have made. Knowing right from wrong, but choosing to do wrong. People that relapse care nothing about rules, and it is easy to see even in recovery. Those that enter into relapse mode start off by being disobedient.

10. <u>Forgetting what it took to get you your freedom</u> – If it's not broken, don't fix it. Meetings, Church, checking in with your sponsor, prayer, fasting and studying the Word of God. These are the things that help you to obtain freedom. Don't abandon them.

11. <u>Boredom</u> – When life becomes uninteresting, we look for other ways of excitement. Sometimes we can talk ourselves into hanging out with old friends thinking this will fix us. Most of the time we look for excitement through external stimuli such as relationships, drugs and alcohol. Those that are on the verge of relapse have slowly severed their relationship with God and are now looking for love, excitement, and fun in all the wrong places.

<u>Drinking and Using Dreams</u>

Recovering people have to also be aware of drunken or using dreams. Dreams that show up early in recovery and can reoccur years later. Reports of drinking and using dreams has occurred 10 or 15 years into the recovery process. When researching these dreams there are several different theories but no concrete answers.

So we would like to add a spiritual expatiation. When reading the chapter on *The Disease of Addiction* we know that addiction centers in our mind, so as long as we can remember there is a chance that alcoholic/addict dreams can happen.

Everyone that we polled had one thing in common the dreams were realistic. Some reported they woke up sweating or shaking afraid they had relapses; others could taste the drug or drink of their choice or not of their choice. Others woke up intoxicated; they felt the effect of the substance.

As we said before there are many theories, but none gave a solution on how to defeat these dreams like Christian Recovery. In Christian recovery there is a very simple solution for this attack by Satan to lead you back to drinking and or using.

For 20 years we operated a Christ-centered in-house treatment center where the men stayed for 9 months to a year. 90% of the participants had reoccurring drinking or drug dreams. When the dream begins we told our clients to simply repeat Jesus name over and over again, the bible says there is power in His name. "Jesus, Jesus, Jesus" is all it takes, and like a bubble popping the dream disappear.

Some believe it was God's power that destroyed the attack from Satan, and others believe it was the client's belief in God's power. Either or in all cases repeating Jesus Name worked!

Chronic Relapsers

In recovery, we also run into what we call the "chronic relapser." They are also known as the "professional recovery person." This person has tried countless times to stop drinking and using. Many of them go in and out of many programs trying to rid themselves of their addiction. There are many reasons why this person fails to capture freedom. The "chronic relapser" is notorious for neglecting responsibility so they avoid these responsibilities by drinking and using. They become experts at going in and out of programs, 6 months here, 9 months there, and in these programs they do well. They hand in all assignments and they adjust to the rules of each program they enter. Inside the programs they are model citizens, they are experts at saying the right thing and convincing their counselors that they are adhering to the program. Their main objective is to stay under the wire and not bring any attention to themselves. They go into each program to rest and regroup, and as soon as they are feeling better, they are off and running again. In the recovery home or in the rooms of recovery they concentrate on looking good by fixing the outside. They spend most of their time working out in the gym, or keeping their hair and nails and clothes intact. In doing this, they are blinded by this obsession to look good in the program, and amongst their peers, missing the program all together. The "professional addict" memories scripture, and the many phrases used in recovery to fool those around him.

Before a "chronic relapser" starts drinking and using, their first order of business is to find a weak woman or a weak man that will buy into the lies and deceit. They need these persons in their lives to lean on while they return to drinking and using. They look for someone of the opposite sex or a loved one to move in with. They look for anyone to pay their bills and not be held responsible. They are experts at say "I love you" catering to a lonely persons needs. All of it is a devious plan to continue drinking and using.

We call the loved ones that support the addicted person a co-dependent or enabler. They are the #1 enemy to the addict/alcoholic's quest for freedom. A co-dependent is a person that un-knowingly assists the addict/alcoholic in their usage. Many co-dependents need "addicts and alcoholics" in their lives to make themselves feel worthwhile. At the same time the "chronic relapser" searches for a co-dependent to fill their need of self worth. They rescue the addict/alcoholic by paying the bills; keep a roof over their head, and food on the table while the addict/alcoholic continues drinking and using. The addict/alcoholic takes advantage of the co-dependents sickness to help someone that is hurting. The co-dependent needs are filled, now they have someone to take care of. Many co-dependents are found in the Church, and they practice their sickness all under the name of "Christian love." This vicious cycle continues until the addict/alcoholic burns all the bridges with the co-dependent can't take it anymore, and finally they sever the ties with the addict/alcoholic. The addict/alcoholic is now forced to get help or find another co-dependent to lean on.

Professional "chronic relapsers" notice that the relationship between themselves and the co-dependent is breaking down, and before it is destroyed, they start looking for someone else to use. I have to pause right here and say, most "chronic relapsers" never sit down and plan this behavior, it is a part of who they are and what they do. Like riding a bike, they do it with out thinking.

The "chronic relapser" can be the most selfish person on planet earth. Unlike the addict/alcoholic that comes into the program for the very first time looking for help, the "chronic relapser" knows what it takes to be free. They just choose not to do what it takes because of their own selfish desires. For the new person coming into the program they have a hard time grasping the disease concept because it's new. They have a hard time understanding that they have to work on themselves daily for change to come about. For the new comer it will be a while before they understand that 5% of their problem is the drugs and alcohol and 95% is the person.

On the other hand, the "chronic relapser" knows and understands this information but they continue to do their own thing. They may say they want to quit drinking and using because they want to get their lives right. They may express freedom to their parents, or they want to be a better husband or wife but these are all part of their plan to get people to trust in them again. The "chronic relapser" is a master manipulator. Their ability to influence others is like second nature to them. It is how they survived in the world they live in.

A person that says he wants to be a marathon runner but never goes to the track to workout is just talking loud, and saying nothing! The "chronic relapser" will say they love their family and are willing to do anything to stay clean and sober, for their family but when it comes to doing the work that it takes to stay clean and sober they have to choose, drugs/alcohol over their family. It takes work to be free and many "chronic relapsers" would rather not do the work. (Therein lies the problem.)

Another problem we see in most "chronic relapsers" is that they have too much information! If it's all the programs they've been in, or being in church all their lives it becomes hard for them to humble themselves and receive again. Once they enter into another program or surrender to another church and the fog begins to lift, what they have learned in pervious programs begins to come back to them and they can't bear to go over this information again. Many dive into the program like a track star running from New York to Los Angeles in 48 hours. They take off at full speed trying to catch up to where they left off the last time they attempted recovery. Most of them tire out before they get to the outskirts of the city. Exhausted, the "chronic relapser" will do what they do best, and that's go into another program to fix the outside and find another co-dependent to help them drink and use.

The same thing happens to the person that looks to the church for help. They stand out because of their knowledge. Quickly they move up in the choir, teacher or minister, and before you know it they can't humble themselves and the disease inside them is released and they slowly affect the auxiliary or ministry their affiliated with until they can't hide their problem. By this time they've borrowed money from every other person in the church. They've found a co-dependent and latched themselves to them and the cycle repeats itself, until too many bridges are burnt and they leave the church.

For the "chronic relapser" the beginning of their battle starts with dealing with their selfishness and self-centeredness. They have to learn to take the "I" out of their conversation. Selfish people have to learn to put the needs of **others** before their own. "Chronic relapsers" have to learn how to take directions if they really want to be free. They have to learn how to put aside everything they know and follow this recovery process to the letter. They have to go back to the meetings and stand up as a new comer, and take the medicine that is prescribed to them. They have to get a sponsor, go to meetings; be willing, open, and honest about who and what they have become. The day they stop taking their medicine the selfishness and the old thinking pattern returns. When working with them always help them to check their motives and why they do the things they do. If they join a gym, ask why? Is it for health reasons or to dress up the outside? Be aware of the material things they accumulate. Are these things do they need or want? The "chronic relapser" can easily be distracted and fooled by Satan's devices.

They must approach each day with a plan, praying that God will give them guidance. The Bible tells us at Matthew 6:35 *"Take no thought for tomorrow for tomorrow will take care of itself."* One day at a time is how we live our lives; when we take on more than that, we enter into a danger zone.

Once you enter recovery, you can't afford to forget that Satan is upset with you for turning your life over to the care of God. Satan knows what you like better than you know yourselves; he surely knows the sin you worshipped, i.e. sexual misconduct, the love of money, etc. The "chronic relapser" must change their lifestyle and fill their mind, body and spirit with fresh new information that will help them to grow in the things of God; or Satan will refund their misery to them.

The bottom line, the addict alcoholic will have to fight for their lives, because if they don't, no one will do it for them. The Bible says in I Peter 5:8, *"Be sober, be vigilant; your adversary the devil walks about like a roaring lion seeking whom he may devour."* Satan's main objective is to send you back to drinking and using, and the pain that you once lived in.

1. In your own words explain Luke 11:24-26.

2. First, give the definition to each word, then give the opposite definition of each word. Next, explain how you can apply this opposite meaning to your life.

A.   **Definition of Frustration**

____

____

B.   **Opposite of Frustration**

____

____

____

3. How would you apply the "opposite answer" to your life?

____

____

C.   Definition of Boldness

____

____

D.   What is the opposite of Boldness

____

____

4. How would you apply your "opposite answer" to your life?

____

____

____

C.   What is the definition of Depression

____

____

D. What is the opposite of Depression

____

____

E. How would you apply your "opposite answer" to your life?

____

____

____

D.   What is the definition of impatience?

____

____

E.   What is the opposite of impatience?

____

____

F. How would you apply the "opposite answer" to your life?

____

____

G. What is the definition of Self-pity?

____

____

H. What is the opposite of Self-pity?

____

____

I. How would you apply the "opposite answer" to your life?

____

____

J. Definition of exhaustion

____

____

K. Opposite of exhaustion

____

L. What causes exhaustion in your life?

____

____

____

M.   Definition of Selfishness?

____

____

N. What is the opposite of Selfishness?

____

____

O. How would you apply the "opposite answer" to your life?

____

____

____

P.   Definition of Boredom

____

____

Q. Opposite of Boredom

____

____

R. How would you apply the "opposite answer" to your life?

____

____

____

Dear Past:

Thank you for your lessons

Dear Future:

I'm Ready

Dear God:

Thank you for another chance!

WHY A SPONSOR

This question will always be asked and has always been asked. Why do I need a sponsor? Why do I have to check in with someone on a daily or weekly basis?

When Bill Wilson and Dr. Bob founded Alcoholics Anonymous, meetings began to spring up all over the nation. Today these meetings occur all over the world. Since 1935, there have been few changes in the structure of AA meetings, the <u>Big Book of Alcoholics Anonymous</u>, or the love of one alcoholic helping another.

No one really knows when that first sober alcoholic, now with clean time, took a newcomer under his/her wings and said, "I will be your sponsor," but many recovering people are grateful that they did. Without the concept of "one addict/alcoholic helping another," Alcoholics Anonymous, Narcotics Anonymous, Cocaine Anonymous, and Free N One, would and could not survive. One addict helping another is therapeutic. There is a special bond between people that have walked the road the new comer is attempting to walk. It's also beneficial to the healing process and at once hope is restored. Recovering people tend to listen to those who have been through the muck and mire that they are walking in now.

When I first graduated from middle school, and was entering into high school, I was so excited about playing football. My buddies and I could not wait for tryouts to begin. On that very first day, we were all disappointed to find out that our new coach was going to be the English teacher who never played football in his life. Over half the team walked off the field demanding the school hire a real football coach. We wanted someone who understood the game being played, and also knew the in's and out's, the ups and downs, and the rights and wrongs of football.

This same principle applies in recovery. When training a person that is recovering from this disease of addiction, many sponsors become excellent counselors. Now I am not saying that a person who has never used drugs or alcohol cannot help a suffering addict/alcoholic find freedom because they can. I am only saying that the addict who is suffering receives the recovering addict/alcoholic who has been addicted, because of their experience.

The hurdle of 'trust' is one of the first hurdles to jump when trying to get a suffering addict/alcoholic to listen to you. In the world of drinking and using, the streets teach the addict not to trust anyone. In recovery, it is easy to trust someone who has walked the same street you have walked and now they are clean and sober. They have something the suffering addict/alcoholic wants freedom.

Another reason recovering addicts and alcoholics make good sponsors is because they know the game that suffering addicts/alcoholics play. They recognize this game because they used to play it themselves. Some suffering addicts have played the game so long they don't realize they are playing a game. It takes someone with clean and sober time who is working a program to point it out and help them correct their sick behavior.

In this recovery process, every "newcomer" is encouraged to seek out someone who has walked this road to recovery and has a personal knowledge of working the steps in their own lives. In the recovery groups, this person is called a sponsor. The recovering person that is seeking help allows the sponsor to take them by the hand and show them how to be free. In turn, after the process of recovery has taken place in the "newcomer's" life, he/she will one day take someone by the hand and help that "newcomer" find freedom him/herself.   It is interesting that in the Bible, this same process was used throughout the Old and New Testament, but the Bible called this person a 'disciple.' Webster defines a disciple as a pupil, a bond by contract or other formal agreement. An agreement is made between the recovering person and the recovering sponsor that has agreed to walk with him/her thought the process of recovery.

A sponsor is someone that has over a year of being clean and sober and has lived the 12 Steps themselves. A "newcomer" that has just started this process called recovery can approach a person who has been in the program clean and sober for at least a year. The "newcomer" is referred to as recovering addicts/alcoholics, but they are "babes" in the program.

It is customary that the men work with the men and the women work with the women, because it is easy for the "babe" to get attached to the sponsor and lose focus on their primary purpose if they are working with the opposite sex.

A sponsor will set some simple rules that the recovering person must follow or else the sponsor has the right to stop working with the "newcomer". Sponsors will attempt to walk the "newcomer" though the group meetings, discuss day-to-day activities, and offer support in understanding and adapting to the 12 Step program. Suggesting that they come out of their comfort zone by greeting people at meetings, shaking their hands and introducing themselves to other people in the program; this just the beginning. Sponsors will take the "newcomer" out to different places around the city, observing their behaviors, teaching simple things like respect, manners, and helping to identify abnormal behaviors. Sponsors sometimes are there to just listen and be a friend to the "newcomer" who is like a child lost in a new world. Sponsors suggest ways for the newcomer to be responsible become accountable and this brings stability back into their lives. The sponsor becomes a friend, but the sponsor has to remember to be honest with the "newcomer," never co-signing (excusing, overlooking or accepting) their abnormal behavior or irregular activities.

Many "newcomers" can't stand this idea of getting a sponsor. They think because they have this new relationship with God that they don't need to check in with anyone. This is just a bad case of a patient fixing himself and not willing to humble themselves to this process. But it even goes deeper. A "newcomer" who won't take suggestions has already entered into relapse mode and soon will return back to their old behaviors, drinking and using.

Another thing to look out for is the "newcomer" that picks a friend to be his or her sponsor. They look for someone that will co-sign their behavior. They look for the Pastor or Deacon or a Evangelist in the Church. We in recovery call this a "Dope-phine moves" they do this knowing that it looks good on the outside but unless the person has applied this Process called Recovery in their lives through the chances are slim to none in them being free from their addiction.

A babe in recovery that selects a person who has at least one year clean and sober and has a working knowledge of the steps is attempting to work a good program because they are following directions.

A sponsor's main objectives are to:

1. Be an honest friend and listen.
2. Guide the recovering person through the process, the 12 Spiritual Steps to Recovery, and let them do the work.
3. Listen to the recovering person and only suggest alternatives to the different situations that will come up in his or her day-to-day life.
4. Never co-sign (excuse, overlook, accept or condone) the recovering person's abnormal or addictive behavior.
5. You see things in that person you want
6. Works the Program in their lives
7. Has a sponsor
8. Has a working knowledge of the Steps
9. Will spend time with you
10. Has a personal relationship with God

For the person looking for a sponsor here are a few things that you want to be cautious of:

1. A person who wants to control your life.
2. A person who is too busy to spend time with you.
3. A person who wants to parade you around as if you were a trophy.
4. A person who has not been through the process. (Worked the steps in their life.)
5. Do not let your pastor, your good friend in the ministry, or your family member be your sponsor. They cannot help you because they have no idea what the process of recovery is about. (Unless they have been through the process themselves.)
6. A person who is not a recovering person. (One addict helping another is therapeutic.)
7. A recovering person who is not practicing the process of recovery and has not been clean and sober for at least one year.
8. A person who does not have a sponsor.

What to look for:

1. A person who will not co-sign (excuse, overlook, accept or condone) everything you say or do. This person must be able to tell you when you are right _and_ when you are wrong.
2. A person who is focused on your growth and not on perfection. As this person gets to know you, he/she will know what you may or may not be capable of achieving.
3. A person who is a coach and not a cop. He/she will encourage you to grow in your weak areas and excel in your strong areas. The person will allow you to make your own mistakes, and when you do, they won't condemn you.
4. A person who loves the Lord. If they love the Lord, they have moral obligations that they live by.
5. A person who is responsible. We look for order in their lives. If they are married, they respect the family institution. If they are going through trials in their marriage, they go through it trusting God. If they are single, they are not playboys or playgirls.

Does this person have a sponsor? A person who has a sponsor humbles himself before men. This person is also teachable and no matter how much "clean or sober" time, he/she finds the potential for growth within themselves. We all have to be accountable to someone. No man is an island.   I consider a sponsor the same way I consider a mother bird taking care of a baby bird. She feeds the baby bird and she encourages him by way of example. One day the mother decides that it is time for that baby to leave the nest. She picks the baby up and drops him out of the nest. It's time to fly. However, the baby is always welcome to return and visit the nest.

The sponsor has to be careful to only make suggestions and not dictate to the "newcomer". This is a time that they must learn how to be responsible, make decisions and, most importantly, change.

Sponsorship can sometimes be very difficult because of the demands of time and energy that some "newcomers" need or ask of the sponsor. They have to be careful not to take on too many "newcomers" because they will not be able give full attention and care. At the same time, the sponsor is working their own program and they must be careful not to build themselves up as saviors; humbling themselves before God at all times.

Sponsors are found at support group meetings where they share their day-to-day experiences during the format of the meetings. A good sponsor is someone who is open and honest about what they going through in life and not afraid to make a mistake in front of a "newcomer" (sponsee). Working out his or her faults in front of the newcomer is good for everyone involved. For the sponsor it helps the newcomer to continue focusing on their program as they keep striving to be a better person in Christ. For the "newcomer" the sponsor gets to see recovery in action. They also witness people that they respect and admire, humbling themselves to God and this process called recovery.

We know that Christian recovery is new to most Churches and congregations. In the beginning, it will be hard to find sponsors. As recovering addicts/alcoholics live free from their disease they are encouraged to make themselves available to the newcomer that is seeking help.

We suggest you pray, believe, and work the process to the best of your ability.   God understands that you are new. He will provide.

1.	Why is a sponsor important?

____

____

2.	What is the purpose of a sponsor?

____

____

3.	Where are sponsors found?

4.   When is a recovering person eligible for sponsoring?

____

5.   What should a sponsor do if a "newcomer" does not want to listen?

____

6.   Why is it dangerous for a sponsor to sponsor too many "newcomers"?

____

____

7.   What happen when a sponsor co-signs the "newcomer's" abnormal behavior?

____

____

____

8.   Why is it dangerous for a male to sponsor a woman, or a woman to sponsor a man?

____

____

9.   Is it good for a sponsor to work out his/her problems in the presence of his sponsee?

☐Yes No ☐

10. Explain. ____

____

For Every Set Back

God

Has a Major Come Back!

WHY SO MANY MEETINGS?
ONE OF THE MOST IMPORTANT PARTS OF
RECOVERY

THE MEETINGS

Working in Christian recovery brings a special challenge to most Christian counselors that believe in the support group concept. The question always asked is, "why?" "Why do I have to go to so many meetings?" Or "Can I just go to Church instead of the meeting?" For some reason even after leaving a residential program many believe they are healed and vow never to return to anything related to recovery. They believe that everything they went through on the streets, drinking and using, combined with nine months to a year in a treatment facility is surely enough punishment, and there is no way they would ever drink or use again.

They disagree that addiction is a disease and it centers in your mind, like a bad cold that comes back if you don't continue taking your vitamins. Even the family members or loved ones buy into this sick thinking and they co-sign the recovering persons idea you don't need meetings. Their lack of knowledge by the family member concerning the process of recovery plays right into the recovering persons hands.

They believe they can watch the recovering person better so they allow them to stay at home, not knowing they are setting them up for relapse.

In my early years working in Christian recovery, I use to think, "Yes you can substitute Bible studies for after-care or Christ-centered meetings." Therefore, we allowed the recovering addict or alcoholic to go to Bible studies during the week instead of Free N One, AA, NA or CA meetings. In tracking our clients, we discovered those that did not attend meetings their success rates fell off tremendously; 98% of them return to drinking and using. Addicts and alcoholics began relapsing at an alarming rate and some were re-admitted into a treatment facility. Clearly, we could see that not going to meetings did not work. Not because Bible studies can't help the recovering person, because we know they can. It is because most Bible studies do not target the special needs of addicts/alcoholics that still have to be addressed.

Quickly we changed our program back to mandatory Christ-centered meetings where our success rate increased. In these meetings, they could talk about this new life they were now attempting to live and hear how the countless others that went before them and succeeded or failed in day-to-day life situations, but they didn't drink or use. They could also ask questions, as they applied the process of recovery in their lives. Unfortunately, or fortunately (depends on how you look at it) some things they have to learn by trial and error, but by coming to the meetings they could share about their experiences and most of the time they find out that they are not by themselves. In the rooms of recovery, someone has walked through what they are now going through.

The addict and alcoholic is a very strange breed and we need special help. Meetings that focus directly with our problem are needed. Structured Christ-centered meetings become the medicine prescribed for this very sick person. It also becomes a safe place to fellowship with people who are just like them. In these rooms they can talk about what may seem normal to those that have never drank or used, but is a giant hurdle to people who are recovering, These rooms are now a safe place and we are not embarrassed to ask questions that we were afraid to ask anyone else. Here we openly share about some of the demoralizing incident that have happened in our past that, if not shared, haunt us every time we attempt to get free. ***(Your secrets will get you loaded.)***

I once invited a sister in the Lord who was an Evangelist from another church to one of my meetings. She had expressed the desire to work in this ministry of drug and alcohol recovery. On the night of the meeting, the room was packed with recovering addicts and alcoholics. This was a three-part meeting: first, we taught on one of the steps; second, is sharing; and third, we bring in a guest speaker. The sharing was so good I was led to cancel the speaker and bring her back the next week. On that night one of the sisters who was a newcomer to the program. She had six weeks six weeks clean and sober and this was the first time she shared. She talked about being a prostitute and described some of the things she did to get drugs. As I looked at my guest, I noticed that she was very uncomfortable as she cried and share some demoralizing things she did to get drugs. The rest of us sat quietly and patiently while this newcomer dumped her heavy and demoralizing load. When the meeting was over the Evangelist could not understand why the sister had to open up in such away. Surely, she didn't think she had to go into detail.

Some of these deep dark secrets are hard to share at Bible studies and Church functions because of guilt and shame. On that night the women in the room who had been down the same road saw what a giant step this newcomer just took and quickly went to embraced her. They new it was difficult to share and they let her know that it was okay. If these secrets stay hidden, Satan has a way of allowing our past to haunt us and we eventually return to using and abusing drugs or alcohol. One of Satan's main tools is guilt. Satan will tell us what we have done in the past is not worthy of forgiveness and God could never love us.   This idea of confessing our sins before men is nothing new to a Christian's walk. When newcomers hear this type of sharing, it allows them to automatically let their guards come down and they, too, are able to talk about the rapes, abandonment, domestic violence, abortions and haunts them daily.

Here are a few more reasons why the addict or alcoholic needs to continue going to meetings:

1. Meetings become a safe place for everyone for the recovering person. Everyone that walks through the door has a story, so the fear of judgment disappears. Nobody stops by our meeting because they have nothing to do.
2. It's biblical. The Bible says at Proverbs 28:13, *"He who covers his sins will not prosper. But whoever confesses and forsakes them will have mercy."* (Also see Psalms 32:5 and 1 John 1:9)
3. To get a recovering person to stand up and share about the TV they stole from their family or the bike that they stole from their kids at Christmas is not an easy thing to do. When they talk about being molested as a child, raped as an adult, or selling their bodies for a hit, the brand new addict who walks into the room for the first time can feel free to let go of whatever is keeping him or her down. In return, they

share, for the first time finding hope and really believing everything will be all right.

4. In the meetings, there are other recovering addicts/alcoholics who understand the process of recovery and are willing to walk with them through this process. One addict helping another is therapeutic.

The "sharing" part of the meeting is not only for releasing past sins, but it is also for dealing with today's trials and tribulations. Addicts and alcoholics specialize in running from responsibilities. Many have done this before they took their first drink or hit. Here we are able to talk about some of these responsibilities and move pass the fear of growing up. In the rooms of recover we get feedback on how to live. It takes a lot of courage to say, "I have never worked on a job, so I don't know how to act" or "I have two kids and I don't know how to be a mother." Once again, the meeting becomes a safe place where we can face our fears. The meetings also become a classroom where they can take what they have heard and now apply it to situations in their life and thus we grow.

The Bible also says we will go through tribulations, meaning unforeseen troubles will come into our lives. Troubles that we have no control over, such as lost of a loved one or friend that can literally crack the very foundation we stand on. When we have no support this becomes the perfect opportunity to return to drinking and using. Even the loved ones are sympathetic to their return to drinking and using. They say things like "Well you know he's got a lot of things on his mind" and they use life's pressures as an excuse to drink and use. Without support from people that have lost loved ones and didn't drink and use, many recovering addicts and alcoholics do return to drinking and using.

We believe that every Church should have some type of drug and alcohol ministry in place. Whether it's a meeting that will allow addicts and alcoholics from all over the city to attend, or it is someone on staff who is equipped to help the addicts or alcoholics in a one-on-one setting; the Church should be a place where hurting people can come and receive special help.

Life without

God ✝

is like an unsharpened pencil ...

there is no **Point**

THE CODEPENTDENT

Take Your God Shoes Off

I once attended a three day conference with individuals that worked in the field of drug and alcohol recovery. At one of the luncheons, we had to answer several questions on a sheet of paper and turn our answers in before lunch was served. One of the questions asked, "What is your biggest hindrance when working with someone addicted to drugs or alcohol addiction?" You would think it would have been the urge to get high or take a drink. Or, letting go of old friends – but, neither was the case. Out of three hundred clinicians, counselors and professionals that work in this field, the number one answer was the "family members and love ones interfering with the recovery process".

Love ones who are unknowingly dismantling the work the counselors are doing while working with the addict/alcoholic. The wife of alcoholics lying to bosses about their husband's missed days at work. The husbands paying off his wife's dope bills because she established a line-of-credit from the drug dealer. The members at the church that tell the addict he can stop going to meetings because he's free in Jesus' name. Or, the grandmother that gets him out of jail again and again and then puts money in his pocket. Many family members believe their love for the addict/alcoholic will override the desire to drink and use.

The Church is notorious for enabling someone that comes to them for help, and many addicts and alcoholics are aware of this. (*Enabling is doing for someone things that they could, and should be doing for themselves*) Addicts/alcoholics find a Church or someone that is "saved" and position themselves to receive the love and help that the church is supposed to offer. (We call them Professional Addicts/Alcoholics.) Christians believe it is their Godly duty to help this person find freedom, but they end up being used by the addict/alcoholic to continue drinking and using. Many go from member to member until their money stream has run out. They burn as many bridges as they can and they move on to another church or another family member.

Addicts and alcoholics are experts at making love ones, friends, or those in the church feel guilty for not helping them. Like a lion looking for its prey, they search for the weakest in the herd, and they attach themselves to them. We call these individuals Codependents. (*Codependents are who they are -- enabling is what they do*) The codependent has this uncontrollable need to help someone and the addict/alcoholic fits the bill. Like a chameleon, the addict becomes whatever they want them to be. They say the right things and for a while will do the right thing, only drawing the codependent in closer until they "fall off the wagon". This is perfect for the codependent. They pick them up, clean them up and try to do better helping them again.

Codependency is defined as a psychological condition or a relationship in which a person is controlled or manipulated by another who is affected with a pathological condition (typically narcissism or drug addiction); and in broader terms, it refers to the dependence on the needs of, or control of, another. [1] It also often involves placing a lower priority on one's own needs, while being excessively preoccupied with the needs of others. Codependency can occur in any type of relationship, including family, work, friendship, and also romantic, peer or community relationships. [2] Codependency may also be characterized by denial, low self-esteem, excessive compliance, or control patterns.

Codependency is a learned behavior usually passed down from someone in their family that was addicted to a bad relationship. Codependents will neglect their own needs to help the addict/alcoholic. Their denial disregards the warnings from family and friends. The codependent's behavior brings dissension between family members who recognizes their sick behavior and those that side with the codependent.

The codependent's low self-esteem stems from their need to be needed which makes the addict/alcoholic a prime candidate. They need someone to take care of them.   In helping the addict/alcoholic they feel good about themselves and it satisfies their need. This falls right into the hands of a practicing addict/alcoholic. Like an angel from dope or alcohol heaven, the codependent is the best thing that has ever happened to the addict/alcoholic. "You're going to save me? Sure, give it a shot" is their thinking. "And when you fail, try, try again".

Most codependents end up becoming very controlling individuals. They control the addict/alcoholic that's in their life and everyone around them. This type of behavior chases many "normal" people away, but not the alcoholic/addict. Being embarrassed and feeling uncomfortable around family and friends is a perfect trade of a place to lay their heads and continue drinking and using.

The codependent dictates the addict/alcoholics every movement. This validates the codependent and builds on their self-esteem while the addict/alcoholic continues drinking and using. When the addict/alcoholic loses total control by drinking and using uncontrollably they return to the codependent to be consoled, and taken care of, promising to do better next time. Ranting and raving means nothing to the addict/alcoholic as long as they have a roof over their heads and the bills are paid.

Once again the codependent drags the addict/alcoholic to church, Bible study, never letting the addict/alcoholic out of their sight. They never let the addict/alcoholic choose life for themselves. The Word of God says *"Come unto me all who labor and are heavy laden and I will give you rest."* God pleads for people to come; twisting their arm is not God's character. God wants them to come freely.

Those that are sheltered by loving parents, or loved ones, never have to face decisions because the codependent makes it for them. For many practicing addict/alcoholics, there is a loved one close by ready to rescue them at a moment's notice, never allowing the addicted person to hit their bottom.

The Bible says, *"Trust in the Lord with all your heart, and lean not to your own understanding".* The codependent has a hard time trusting God in this area because they believe they are called by God to help the practicing addict/alcoholic find freedom. They continue to pray for the addict/alcoholic but their belief is far from their action.

Loneliness plays a big part in the codependent's need to take care of someone. To the codependent, half of nothing is better than nothing at all. But is it really? Once the addict/alcoholic enters into treatment and the recovery process begins to change the addict/alcoholic's life, freedom begins to take place in other areas as well.

The now recovering addict/alcoholics is taught to "Trust in God" so they no longer need the codependent. 95% of my clients divorce after finding freedom. They no longer have to put up with the sick controlling ways of the codependent. This is why we suggest the codependent receive help during this time. The codependent can be just as sick as the addict/alcoholic.

If you believe God can fix this problem -- then let Him. God does not need your help! Some addicts/alcoholics may have to visit the local jail, live on the streets, or, be separated from their families because of their disobedience. If you're praying for their freedom, then believe in the prayer you have prayed. Turn them over to God and let God fix it, because your way is obviously not working. Trust me; God can do a better job than you!

To those codependents that believe the Word of God and you have been praying for that loved one's freedom, *"Take Your God Shoes Off"*! You are in the way of what God wants to do in that person's life. Continue to pray for them and their protection but that's all you can do. God has a plan for their life, and God needs their full attention.

Why should a person addicted to drugs or alcohol look to God if they can time after time look to you? Mother you are their God, father you are not their savior, wives and husbands you are the one they look to for help instead of all mighty God!

I know this is difficult for many but there is help for you. We at Free N One Drug and Alcohol Program can help you. We have a program entitled, "Tough Love." Tough Love is a group of individuals that have walked down your path and found peace in the midst of the storm. In these rooms they learn how to take a good look at themselves. The denial, low-self esteem, the controlling behavior is all uncovered. The now recovering codependent will receive tool that will help them deal with all the drama, all the lies and challenges that come with loving a person addicted to drugs or alcohol. In the rooms of "Tough Love," they learn how to set boundaries and say no.

The quicker you *Take Your God Shoes Off* and get out of the way, the faster God can begin working on that person you've been praying for!

Chapter **III**

UNDERSTANDING THE 12 STEP PROCESS

The 12 Steps to Recovery are simple guidelines that put order into a life that is filled with confusion. First, this process meets the recovering person right where they are and slowly leads them through a process that will change their lives forever. Second, the steps keep you focused on your road to recovery and acts as a road map to healing.

It is very hard to say how long a person should work on each step because each step will be different for each person, and each step will present a different hurdle. The minimum time spent on each step is at least two months.

It is suggested that the "newcomer" takes suggestions from someone that has gone through the process of recovery and these 12 Steps. Once again, there is no time limit on when you should finish these steps. (Easy does it, but do it.) But "do it" is the key; putting one foot in front of the other.

Once you start this process there is no turning back, you must learn how to finish what you have started, always striving to get better in your recovery? Living this program everyday of your life is the key to growth; standing still is not an option. We must continue to move forward in this process. *(Keep pressing towards the mark of the high calling in Christ Jesus.)*

12 Spiritual Steps to Recovery

1. We admitted that we could not control our addiction and our lives became unmanageable. (Romans 7:15-25)

2. Learned to believe that God can and will restore us to a right relationship with Him through Jesus Christ. (Matthew 11:28-30, Romans 3:22-23, Romans 5:9-10)

3. Made a quality decision to let God have complete control over our will and lives through His Word. (Joshua 24:15, Psalms 119:4, Proverbs 3:5-6, Matthew 6:24, 33)

4. Made a thorough and fearless moral examination of ourselves on paper. (2 Corinthians 13:5)

5. Confessed to God in the name of Jesus, admitted to ourselves, and unashamedly admit the exact nature of our wrongs to another human being. (Proverbs 28:13, James 5:16, 1 John 1:9)

6. Became entirely ready to have God take away all these blocks to our freedom in Christ. (Galatians 5:1, Hebrews 12: 1,2, Psalms 86:10-13, Psalms 119:57-59)

7. Humbly asked God in the name of Jesus and thanked Him for His mercy and for giving us the strength to overcome our faults. (John 16:24, 1 Peter 5: 6-10, James 4:10, Psalms 51:10, Psalms 19:12-14)

8. Wrote down all those persons we had harmed and became willing to make restitution to them all. (Matthew 5:23-24, Luke 19:8-10)

9. Made direct restitution to such persons whenever possible except when to do so would injure them or others. (James 5:16 Luke 6:31, 36-37)

10. Examined ourselves daily to see if we are being doers of the Word and not just hearer only. If wrong promptly confess it. (James 1:22, James 5:16, 1 John 1:8-10, Ephesians 4:26)

11. Continue to pray, study and meditate on the Word, and maintain consistent fellowship with believers, to improve our relationship with God. (Joshua 1:8, Psalms1:1-3, 1 Thessalonians 5:17, 2 Timothy 2:15, Hebrews 10:25)

12. Having had a born again experience, and having been freed from our addiction, we shared our testimony with those who are still in bondage and continued to be doers of the Word in all our affairs. (Matthew 28:19-20, Romans 1:16, Galatians 5:1 and 13, 1 Timothy 6:18, John 3:3)

Step 1

We admitted that we could not control our addiction and our lives became unmanageable. (Romans 7:15-25)

Step #1 is the beginning of recovery. If we cannot admit that we have a problem, then we might as well go back to living in pain and torment. If we cannot admit that our lives have become unmanageable, then we will never start this process off in the right direction nor recover from this illness. People that never admit they have a problem are in what clinicians refer to as denial. They deny they have a problem, they deny that their life is unmanageable they deny that anything is seriously wrong. When trying to work with a person who is in denial, most of the time you are wasting your time, their time, and the time of everyone involved. The addict/alcoholic must recognize that they have a problem before serious recovery can begin.

When an addict/alcoholic admits he or she has a problem, they have begun the most important work that they will ever do towards their recovery, and that is surrender. No more hiding, no more sneaking, no more acting like your okay, and no more attempts to stay clean on your own. For most of us, admitting that we have no power and no control is no easy task. No one wants to admit to being weak and out of control. When you took your first drink or hit, your plan was not to be an addict or alcoholic. No one plans to be separated from families and friends, and most of all, separated from God. Once we get honest with ourselves, we realize something is very wrong and our lives are unmanageable. Once we surrender to the fact we are out of control and need help, we now have to allow God to guide us through this process called recovery.

This first step meets every practicing addict/alcoholic where they are. You do not have to live on Skid Row to qualify for this step; you can be married with children, single and in school, or live in a mansion in Beverly Hills. If you are drinking and/or using has gotten out of control, it is time to consider the first Step. The first step speaks to your innermost soul and an honest answer is all that is needed. You may be able to fool some of the people some of the time, and most of the people most of the time, but you can't fool yourself or God none of the time.

Denial is no longer a problem when you have tried everything in your power to stop, but you continue to drink and use anyway. Family members tell you, "you may have a problem with drinking or using," or friends have said things like "don't you think you had enough?" However, you kept right on drinking or using. To you they were just being nosey and should mind their own business, but slowly, even you were starting to notice signs of being out of control. Surely, you didn't believe you were an alcoholic or an addict, and seeking treatment was out of the question. What is there to fix if you don't think anything is broken? You continue to drink and use and like the song says, "you can't hide from yourself –

everywhere you go there you are." Finally, you have to face the fact that something is desperately wrong. Convinced there is a problem, in your own feeble way you try to control your drinking or using, but by this time, it is too late. It's like trying to stop a run-away train with no brakes going down hill on a snowy day! Once you surrender to the fact that you have a problem, staying convinced will be the next hurtle.

The disease of addiction has an uncanny way of making the individual forget just how bad the problem really is or was. This is one reason you keep coming back to meetings. In the rooms of recovery, you are constantly reminded that the disease of addiction is alive and well.

Here at Step 1, we realize that the practicing addict/alcoholic has no clue on how to stay clean and sober. We suggest that you take a very good look at your relationship with drugs and alcohol, and what it has done to you. When we began drinking and using, the troubles of life intensified. Those who are honest with themselves and look back at their relationship with drugs and alcohol will see nothing but destruction during this period of their drinking and using.

Going to meetings, selecting a sponsor, and studying your Bible will be the first assignments asked of you on your road to recovery. Once you throw up the white flag and surrender, you must learn how to trust someone who has been through this process called recovery. Sharing with your sponsor and your new Christian friends that also attend recovery meetings will help you in your growth during this first step.

Honesty will be the addict's/alcoholics next big hurdle. Like eating and sleeping, telling a lie goes hand in hand with drinking and using. Once you get honest with God and with yourself, you are on the road to freedom. For some it becomes easy. They recognize that they are on the bottom of this thing called life and they are willing to go to any length to be free; so they are willing to get what we call being "butt naked honest," holding back nothing. They are willing to shed everything and start all over again hiding nothing. In order to do this you have to swallow all pride and stand before God and your peers transparent. Those that start this new live on the wrong road will eventually they find themselves lost again drinking and using.

Those who take advantage of this new beginning recognize that they are liars and cheats and can't be trusted. We know this is hard but the truth hurts and we are not here to baby anyone. If you tiptoe around honesty, "your misery will be refunded back to you." Can anybody tell me just what are you trying to hold on to, acting like you're not that bad? The white flag has to come up if freedom is going to begin. Surrender to a life right with God because it's the only thing left, except for death. You have tried everything else. From here, all you can do is go up.

Then there are those who come into this process holding onto what little dignity they think they have left. They always look for someone worst off than them. After a few months clean and sober their pride puffs them up and their better-than spirit walks them right out of the door. Allow God to strip you of everything so this new person can begin this fresh new walk in Christ. It is not mandatory that you lose everything, but some of us do. Those that come into recovery thinking that they are better than others or not as bad as others have a hard time seeing themselves because they are looking at everyone else.

We must recognize that it is God and only God who can restore us to sanity. In some cases, not being stripped of everything can be a problem. Once the pain is gone, and you add a few possessions to your life, suddenly you are not teachable anymore; now you are an accident ready to happen. It is so easy to be tricked by Satan into thinking that you are not that bad. Unfortunately, when you regain power, you loose humility. You end up forgetting where your came from, using drugs and alcohol again and having to start this process all over again if you're lucky. When we humble ourselves, we understand that it is God that spared us from losing everything, and it is God that will keep us in the right frame of mind.

Also, here at the first step you have to learn about the disease of addiction. We could throw statistic at you or tell you that every major medical association known to man considers addiction a disease. We would rather show you the disease in operation in the Bible.

This next scripture is one of the most powerful scriptures in the Bible concerning bondage, it links honesty and powerlessness to what the practicing addict/alcoholic goes through daily. What is interesting about this scripture, Paul the writer, was not a babe in Christ when he wrote this. By the time he arrived in Rome, 15 years had passed since his experience on the road to Damascus. He was a true man of God, yet this is how he felt.

Paul states in Romans 7:15-25, *(New Living Translation)*[15] *"I don't understand myself at all, for I really want to do what is right, but I don't do it. Instead, I do the very thing I hate.* [16] *I know perfectly well that what I am doing is wrong, and my bad conscience shows that I agree that the law is good.* [17] *But I can't help myself, because it is sin inside me that makes me do these evil things.* [18] *I know I am rotten through and through so far as my old man is concerned. No matter which way I turn, I can't make myself do right. I want to, but I can't.* [19] *When I want to do good, I don't. And when I try not to do wrong, I do it anyway.* [20] *But if I am doing what I don't want to do, I am not really the one doing it; the sin within me is doing it.* [21] *It seems to be a fact of life when I want to do what is right, I inevitably do what is wrong.* [22] *I love God's law with all my heart.* [23] *But there is another law at work within me that is at war with my mind. This law wins the fight and makes me a slave to the sin that is still within me.* [24] *Oh what a miserable person I am. Who will free me from this life that is dominated by sin?* [25] *Thank God. The answer is in Jesus Christ our Lord. So you see how it is: In my mind I really want to obey God's law, but because of my sinful nature I am a slave to sin."*

This is a classic example of what alcoholics and addicts goes through daily. Paul is controlled by and/or addicted to some type of sin and is unable to stop doing what he is doing, under his own power. We thank God that Paul never told us what he was struggling with. If Paul had shared what this problem was, we would think that deliverance could only happen in that particular area. However, in God's infinite wisdom, He did not tell us what Paul was going through. So now, anyone who is struggling with any type of addiction can find freedom in knowing that a man who wrote thirteen books of the Bible went through what they are going through now. This section of scripture applies to anyone who is having a problem trying to be free.

Satan does not care how strong you are or how much of a man you think you are; we all need God's Power to keep us from falling. In the area of drug and alcohol addiction, we need Jesus even more. (This is a perfect time to ask God to come into your heart.)

We must also remember that this is a spiritual warfare No matter what plan you try to put together, your fight will be fruitless without God. The Bible tells us in II Cor. 10:3-5, *"For though we walk in the flesh, we do not war after the flesh: For the weapons of our warfare are not carnal, but mighty through God to the pulling down of strong holds;*

Casting down imaginations and every high thing that exalteth itself against the knowledge of God, and bringing into captivity every thought to the obedience of Christ."

You can try to fight this battle on your own if you want to, but sooner or later, you end up right back where you started, on the bottom again! This is why some programs state, "once you are an addict, you are always an addict." We tend to believe "once you are an addict, you are a recovering addict." There is a difference.

Learning to be powerless will play a big part in a recovering person's life as he grows in recovery.   Learning to be powerless means you are putting your whole life into God's hands and He can do whatever He wants with it. The Bible says in Isaiah 64:8, *"Yet O Lord, you are our Father. We are the clay, you are the potter; we are all the work of your hand."* You have to be willing to let God do what he wants to do in your life.

Here in the beginning, at Step 1, a change must take place, and we must allow God to orchestrate this change. In our many attempts to rid ourselves of our addiction, our main goal was to stop using. Today we know that this can only happen when our thinking, our behavior, and who we serve changes. We have a saying in Free N One, "When there is no change, there is no change." If you do not change, you remain the same. Living the same way you used to live, doing the same things you used to do, yet expecting different results, is insanity.

It takes power to change, a power greater than you. If an addict could save himself then he would have done it long time ago and he wouldn't be in the position he is in today. Learning how to depend on God for everything takes a made up mind, a renewed mind, and a mind that is stayed on God.

The key to obtaining this power starts at becoming powerless. You have t understand that you can't fix your life. Powerlessness does not mean power will not be in your life. Power will come, but God will give it to you and it is His power, God's power. We get this twisted, we mix this up, thinking that we have something to do with it. NO! GOD HAS TO GET THE GLORY! So remember, it's God's power that lives in us. Not your power. The Bible says in James 4:10, *"Humble yourselves in the sight of the Lord, and He will lift you up."* Understand this concept and you will continue to grow by leaps and bounds. When you surrender to God, God will empower you to get His work done. You may ask why is this so important to God. It is found in Isaiah 14:12-14, *'How you are fallen from heaven, O lucifer, son of the morning.   How you are cut down to the ground. You who weakened the nations. (13) For you have said in your heart: I will ascend into heaven, I will exalt my throne above the stars of God; I will also sit on the mount of the congregation. On the farthest sides of the north; (14) I will ascend above the heights of the clouds, I will be like the Most High."* Of course, we know that lucifer tried to exalt himself above God because of whom he thought he was. But look how many times lucifer says "I". This sounds like every addict or alcoholic that has ever lived. "I don't need any help, I can do this on my own, I can quit when I want to. I don't need to go to any meetings, I don't need a sponsor, I'm a good teacher, I'm a good preacher, "I", "I", "I". God has a problem with "I". Lucifer was kicked out of heaven and sent to the lowest hell because of "I." Today God still has a problem with "I". God must get the glory because He is God, the author and the finisher of our faith and the director of our lives. We as Christians must acknowledge God as Chief Director in everything we do.

By the time we surrender at Step 1, we are looking at an impossible situation. As you grow and study the Word, you will find out that God does His best work in impossible situations. It is as if God waits until we have exhausted every avenue. (Become powerless) or ("I can't do it.") Once we have no more fight left, God steps in and allows us to witness His power.

Powerlessness works in all aspects of a recovering person's life. It allows the recovering person to let other people be who they are. When operating in a powerless state, we learn that we cannot control other people, places or things. We have to let people make their own mistakes in life and allow them to live their own lives.

We learn to be powerless over stressful situations that occur in our own lives. This teaches us that things do happen that are out of our control (welcome to life). In our addiction, we got high or drank about life's situations. The pressures of life were too much for us (not enough power). Today, because of powerlessness, we have learned how to take a deep breath, surrender to God and use whatever tools He has prepared for us in this process, and not be mentally affected by life's situations. Powerlessness teaches us humility and patience, which helps us to think first instead of making rash decisions that usually are bad decisions. Thinking first may sometimes have you to *be still and know that he is God*. We are learning how to get out of the way and let God do what He is going to do. Understanding the whole concept of being powerless allows the recovering person to live with peace, giving God all the Glory.

Through God's grace, powerlessness allows the recovering person to witness God's miracles as they learn to step out of the way and behold the power of God. Once you admit you have a problem, you are also saying you can no longer manage your life. You can no longer be the adult you once thought you were and you need God's help; and because God works through people, so be it! One thing is sure; you can't stay free on your own. To take this step at face value, once you read this step and say "yes" I admit I have a problem and my life is unmanageable, it would seem you are ready for the next step. Nothing is further away from the truth. We now begin looking at what brought us to the point of using drugs or alcohol. We know that only 5% of the problem is the drugs or alcohol and 95% of the problem is the individual. (Look in the mirror and welcome yourself to the problem.) Step 1 will be something you practice for the rest of your life.

The question that many people ask and don't understand is "how do I live this step for the rest of my life"? There are 3 things that anyone beginning this process has to incorporate in their life, and that is *Honesty, Open Mindedness, and Willingness.*

Honesty

First start with *Honesty*, one of the addict/alcoholics biggest problem when walking through the doors of recovery. Being honest with themselves is the beginning of recovery. Looking in the mirror and seeing the problem daily will be the hardest part of the first step. This is why anyone that has walks this road call recovery will tell you to make plenty of meetings. In these meetings you will you will see yourself in the dysfunction of others. You witness recovering people overcome their faults. Faults that you refuse to admit in your own life.

Telling the truth is next. Lying is a major part of being an addict/alcoholic. We lied about drinking and using or how much we drank or used. We lied to get more drugs; we lied to get more money to get more drugs or alcohol. We deceive or tried to deceive our love ones and employers only to find out that we were deceiving our selves.

Who is the real you will be the question you have to ask yourself. Many walk through the doors and have a hard time answering the question. The world of drugs and alcohol is filled with lies and deception, and lies and deception is how you get in.

Open Mindedness

Having an *Open mind* is next. The reason you sought help your way was not working. The pain of stopping and starting, going cold turkey and relapsing is now unbearable. Don't come into the program asking for help and deny the help that has worked for millions of people. We understand that change is hard but remember "when there is no change, there is no change"!

When I first came into the program they told me to "take the cotton out of my ears and stick it in my month". I had to learn how to listen and take some of the suggestions from people that was free.

To my Christian friends that come into the program. Remember you were doing your best thinking and you ended up an addict/alcoholic, so give yourself a break and let this process work for you. Take what you think you know and sit it on the shelf. You will be able to use most of it at a later date. If you believe God has ordered your steps then God led you to this process. Let it happen for you.

Willingness

Willingness takes courage. Courage to step out of your comfort zone, (and by the way nothing is no longer comfortable), and try something new. Willingness ask for action. Be willing to change. Be willing to take direction, be willing to surrender to this process called recovery. Be willing to go to meetings, be willing to follow God as you understand him. Willingness will go against the bad habits you've created in your life.

Those that struggle at willingness struggle with recovery and tend to be chronic relapsing individuals.

What specific areas in your life must you admit you have no control over and have become unmanageable? For the addict and alcoholic there is more than one area. This is why it takes a while to move on to the next step. Once you get started, you will find that you take this step with you everywhere you go. You never get off of Step 1.

1.   Why is the first Step so important?

____

____

2.   Why must the addict/alcoholic admit he/she has a problem?

____

____

3.   Explain Roman 7:15 – 25 and what it means to you? (Explain fully.)

____

____

4.   When did you first know that you had a problem and what happened?

____

____

____

____

5.   When you start your first step what will you have to give up? (There's more than

one answer)

____

____

6.   If there were one area in your life that is unmanageable, that you could change at
this moment, what would it be? Why? (Do not include drug/alcohol addiction
remember honesty is the key.)

____

____

____

7.   What other areas besides drugs and alcohol have you attempted to control?
(People, places, and things.)

____

____

____

8.	In this chapter, we talk about having a made up mind. What does this mean to you?

____

____

9.	At this point, what causes you to seek help with your drug and alcohol problem? (Was there one incident or many?) (Explain fully.)

____

____

10.	Have you ever tried to run from your addiction, moving from neighborhood to neighborhood, and city-to-city, or state-to-state? Yes ☐ No ☐

11.	If yes, what happened when you arrived at this new location? _______________

____

____

12.	How many times does Lucifer say "I" in Isaiah 14:12-14? ____________

13.	Why does God have a problem with men using "I" in their sentence?

____

____

14.	Why does powerless play such a big part in Step 1?

____

____

15.	Why is honesty so important?

____

____

16.	What does "butt naked honesty" mean?

____

____

17.	What was the hardest thing for you to get honest about and why?

____

____

____

18.	In your own world explain Open-mindedness, and Willingness

____

____

____

____

____

____

____

STEP 2

Learned to believe that God can and will restore us to a right relationship with Him through Jesus Christ. (Matthew 11:28-30, Romans 3:22-23, Romans 5:9-10)

Once you understand Step 1, you begin to apply it in your life. It is time to look for positive alternatives toward living. By now, you are totally convinced that you cannot control this addiction and cannot stop when you want to. As the white flag of surrender flies in the hearts and minds of those who realize that there is no human power that can relieve them of the disease called addiction, you are introduced to a power that can free you from this vicious way of living in this dungeon you call life. In this dungeon - you existed day-to-day instead of living victoriously in Christ Jesus. In Step 2, you will meet the God that has been secretly working on your behalf while you were lost and out of control, keeping you safe and guiding you to this point. Oh yes, God has been with you all the time. It may be hard to see at this point because you are still in a fog and you have a hard time seeing pass the wreckage of your past, but believe me, it is only by God's grace that you are still alive.

Here at Step 2, you will begin your relationship with Jesus Christ. II Timothy 2:15, *study to show thy self approve unto God, a workman that needeth not to be ashamed, rightly dividing the word of truth.* It is here that you will begin to understand God's likes and God's dislikes, and most importantly, how much God loves you. You will begin to separate fact from fiction, right from wrong, and fantasy from reality. The Word tells us in John 8:32 that *"you shall know the truth and the truth shall make you free."*

There are three groups of recovering people that meet here at Step 2. The first group was introduced to God at a very young age, where God-centered principles were taught in the home, and God was given the glory. This group understands God as the higher power whether they accepted the philosophy or not. They were forced or willingly went to Church, and religion was a part of the home structure.

The second group knows of God and believes there is a God but were never formally introduced to or avoided religion and any formal commitment altogether. This group believes there is a God but is not ready to commit or surrender to Him or more importantly the lifestyle that goes along with it. By the time they walk through the doors of recovery they surrender easily, but, like the other two groups, struggle with the lifestyle. (Living righteous and holy)!

The third group knows nothing about God or religion, only what they heard in the streets and most of this was negative. By the time they walk through the doors of recovery they feel they have nothing to lose because their way of life certainly didn't work for them, and if Jesus is presented in a favorable light, this is better than what they have at this present moment.

For the first group that was introduced to God at an early age, they recognized the power of God by personal experience, witness, or testimony. They believe God can save, deliver, and heal others; but, because of many failed attempts to be free from their addiction, they have a problem believing that this miracle can happen for them. Some believe God is upset with them because of their disobedience and this is their punishment. Others believe that they have not put forth enough effort, so they totally surrendered to God, try to make more Bible studies, and surely make it to Church on Sunday. The biggest stumbling block is they believe that they are bad people trying to be good, instead of sick people trying to get well. In their attempt to evaluate just what went wrong in their lives, they believe it boils down to the bad choices they made and the bad people they hung out with. In most cases, they're right but they never factor in that they have a sickness that has to be treated. So, in their many attempts to be "good people," they forget that the Bible says that they can never be good enough. Out of the three groups, this group relapses more. They have a problem grasping the disease concept.

The second group believes there is a God but because of holiness and righteousness were never taught in their family structure, their sinful nature runs wild and they see living as a Christian as being boring and dull or unreachable. The only thing that keeps them close to God is their continued roller-coaster ride through life; always calling on God to bring them out when the roller coaster is down in the valley. Once God brings them out and they can see above the pain and suffering, they leave God and try to handle life on their own once again. This group has a hard time believing you need God in every step of your life. Proverbs 3:5-6 *says "Trust in the Lord with all thy heart and lean not to thine own understanding, in all thy ways acknowledge Him and He will direct thy path."* The disease of addiction tells them that their willpower is enough and all that they have accomplished was because of hard work and dedication.

There are many ways to "learn to believe" here at Step 2. Everyone learns at his or her own pace and in different ways. What is good about Step 2 is that God will meet you where you are. First, you have to learn how to learn. We have to become and stay teachable, reachable, and keep an open-mind. Here we find out there is a difference between reading and studying the Word of God. The Bible tells us at II Timothy 2:15, *"study to show thy self approve unto God, a workman that needed not to be ashamed, rightly dividing the word of truth."* Once you start studying God's Word, it will take you deeper into the heart and spirit of our Lord and Savior Jesus Christ. The Bible says at *John 1:1, "In the beginning was the Word, and the Word was with God, and the Word was God."* This tells us that inside the Word, is God, and as we study God's Word, we understand God. The second part of this learning process is stepping out on faith, and doing some of the things that God has asked us to do in His Word. Here we have to "take action" or "participate in our own recovery." We take action by applying what we are learning in God's Word and this process called recovery to our lives. From here on out, it takes work on the recovering person's part. These faith-taking steps might be very foreign to you, and surly is different from anything you have done before. For example, consistently going to meetings and participating in them, and getting involved in your recovery. Religiously going to Bible studies to understand the Word of God. Changing where you play and your playmates. Making new friends and being willing to take on this new life style, now that's stepping out on faith!

Giving of your time, changing your friends and where you used to play, is all a part of this learning process. This will take not only faith but also courage. It takes faith to step out, and courage to change. For the new person in recovery, you were doing your best thinking and you became an alcoholic/addict. Its time you learn to take some suggestions. Here at Step 2 we begin the change from insanity to sanity. One writer's definition of insanity is "doing the same thing over and over again expecting different results." Here at step 2 we have to make up our minds to change, and to trust people that have walked this road before us. When I first came through the program, I learned by watching clean and sober people go through this process. God works through people, and there is nothing wrong with imitating others. Dr. Jeremiah Wright of Trinity United Church of Christ in Chicago has a saying "It's OK to be a copy cat as long as you copy the right cat." In the rooms of recovery, you will see things in people that you like and you dislike, and you can learn from both. From those that you like you take away what they do, and how they do it. You even get there phone numbers so you can ask them question about this new walk. The Bible says *Iron sharpens iron.* For those people in the program that may rub you the wrong way, you can learn from them also. If they are disrespectful, rude loud, saying one thing and doing another, or whatever the case may me, you tell yourself "I don't want what they have" and you try to live your life pleasing to God and yourself. As we surrender our will, and accept God's will, we begin to see God working in our lives and that He has our best interest at heart. *Matthew 11:28 -30 says, "Come unto me, all ye that labor and are heavy laden, and I will give you rest. Take my yoke upon you, and learn of me; for I am meek and lowly in heart: and ye shall find rest unto your souls. For my yoke is easy and my burden is light."* Here God calls everyone who is loaded down with any kind of burden (drugs and alcohol addiction) to bring those burdens to Him. God wants our problems, our pains, and our sickness. We must learn how to turn our cares and our burdens over to Christ. In stepping out on faith and giving God this pain that we have been holding on to for so long, we must turn doubt and fear into trust and faith, learning how to give everything to God and leave it with Him. Once you begin to "Try God," you will see how much God loves you. When we were practicing our disease, we turned our back on God. One writer wrote, "We left God, God never left us."

Joshua 1:5 reads, *"No one will be able to stand up against you all the days of your life as I was with Moses, so I will be with you; I will never leave you nor forsake you."* I will never leave you or forsake you; this is a powerful and encouraging statement made by a God that really loves us. For most of us, if we take a good look at our past we will see that God has been with us the whole time. God has brought us out of not just one but many dangerous situations. Many of us come to God battered, beaten down and confused, without any hope, and some worse than others. The only one who can pick you up, dust you off, and give back your hope is Christ Jesus. The 2nd Step says, "Learn to believe that God can and will restore us to a right relationship with Him." Develop a personal relationship with the Lord. Know God for yourself. Pray morning, noon, and night, and God will reveal Himself to you.

Working in this ministry, I have found that Step 2 is where many newcomers get stuck, and eventually this is where they relapse. Some have a problem being teachable. Others have a problem with trusting and having faith in what they read in the Bible or hear from the pulpit; stories such as Jesus walking on water or God parting the Red Sea, or maybe it's seeing someone get the Holy Ghost and fear or disbelief enters in. Instead of faith-walking, they try and rationalize what they are hearing with their own thinking. They have forgotten that it was this same thinking that got them into recovery in the first place. Here, you have to surrender daily and trust that the same God that protected you from a certain death and now has you in a safe place; knows what He is doing. When your mind comes up with another plan, remember that your mind is not always your friend and that your thinking is broke! Share your thoughts with others who have walked this road and who will not co-sign your madness.

Everyday in your prayer sincerely ask God to make Himself real to you. In time, God will reveal Himself and you will never question God again. Also, think back to the times you escaped danger and the only reason you are alive today is because of a miracle. Some of us have been shot, cut, raped, kidnapped, or have overdosed on drugs and God brought us out.   Some of us drank so much that we experienced blackouts, not knowing what happened the night before or who you where with. Waking up safely at home, not knowing how we got home, or where we were the night before. Sometimes it seems as if our cars automatically drove themselves home. Or maybe you never had these experiences but you lost just about everything along with your self-respect and now God is giving you another chance. Don't forget God!

Some say it is luck, but we who have come to believe that God can do all He said He could know otherwise. Do understand that it was God's grace that watched over us while we were in our addiction. It was God's grace and mercy that kept us. If you look closely, you will see miracles that happened and are happening in your own life. No it wasn't God parting the Red Sea--or was it?

Once God reveals Himself to you, you must work on developing a personal relationship with Him. This work is never ending. Until Jesus comes back or until we die, we must continue working on perfecting our relationship with God. For example, the day before Martin Luther King, Jr. died he shared something that the world will never forget. In his speech he said, "Mine eyes have seen the glory of the coming of the Lord." He went on to say, "I may not make it to the mountain top with you, but as a people we will all make it to the mountain top." At the time, everyone thought this was just another great speech by Martin Luther King, Jr. Martin was killed the very next day by an assassin's bullet. He knew his time was up and he was going home to be with the Father. What type of relationship did he have with God?   What type of relationship did he have that God would show him a vision in a dream? Do you want that type of relationship? Well you can have that type of relationship only if you believe!

"I press towards the mark for the prize of the high calling of God in Christ Jesus." (Philippians 3:14) Always strive to better your relationship with God.

Whatever the case may be, "learning to believe that God can" and "being patient until He does it" will be the obstacles for everyone entering recovery. We know that before you get too deeply into the second Step, the disease is already telling you that you don't need these steps or this new life with God. For some, by the time you get to the second Step you may have 60 to 90 days clean and your head is telling you if you can stay clean for this amount of time you can make it for the rest of your live. Of course, that is ridiculous, the disease is alive and well in your mind; if you don't continue taking your medicine, applying the process of recovery into your life, going to meetings and participating you are on your way to a fall.

Many understand that the process is just beginning; now you must change your life and learn how to trust in almighty God. Stepping out on faith will help you to develop a solid foundation in Him. Step 2 is more than just reading the Word of God, it's trying God's Word in your life and learning for yourself that He is real. Remember you were doing your best thinking and you ended up hooked on drugs or/and alcohol, now it's time to give God a chance.

1. What group best describes you? (Check one)

   A. You were taught God at an early age. ☐

   B. You heard about God but never were you formally introduced to Christ, or have never accepted Christ into your life. ☐

   C. The only God you ever heard of was in the streets. ☐

2. Have you considered giving up this process of recovery and moving on with your life?
   Yes ☐   No ☐

3. If "yes" what is making you continue with this process?

   ____

   ____

4. What is the difference between reading and studying?

   ____

   ____

5. How will **you** personally "try God"? (This phase is an "action" phase. Think about it and give an honest answer.)

   ____

   ____

6. How do you work on bettering your relationship with God? List those ways."

   ____

   ____

7. How is Matthew 11:28-30 applied to your life?

____

____

8. Summarize Step 2. What does it mean to you?

____

____

____

____

Step 3

Made a quality decision to let God have complete control over our will and lives through His Word. (Joshua 24:15, Psalms 119:4, Proverbs 3:5-6, Matthew 6:24, 33)

Making a quality decision means having a made-up mind to follow God and living the Word of God to the best of your ability. Making a quality decision means not only making God our Savior, but also making him Lord of our lives. Once God is Lord of our lives, we bow down before him in awe of His love, His power, and His presence. At Step 3, we have made up our minds to trust God.

Matthew 6:24 says, "No man can serve two masters, for either he will hate the one, and love the other; or else he will hold to the one, and despise the other Ye cannot serve God and mam'-mon." (Mam-mon represents money or things.) There are many Christians addicted to drugs, alcohol, or just sin, who are trying to prove this scripture wrong. They spend years trying to master these two worlds to no avail. Living as a Christian by going to church, singing in the choir, working on the usher board; they continue all their "Christian" responsibilities. But they have another life where they find worldly pleasures that are controlled by Satan, never thinking they will be trapped and have a hard time getting out. This scripture lets us know that you will not be able to juggle both worlds.

Joshua 24:14-15 *14 "Now fear the LORD and serve him with all faithfulness. Throw away the gods your forefathers worshiped beyond the River and in Egypt, and serve the LORD . 15 But if serving the LORD seems undesirable to you, then choose for yourselves this day whom you will serve, whether the gods your forefathers served beyond the River, or the gods of the Amorites, in whose land you are living. But as for me and my household, we will serve the LORD ."* Here Joshua has a made up mind and pledges his allegiance to our Lord and Savior. There is no question to where his loyalty lays.

Here at Step 3 we have to learn to trust God. *Proverbs 3:5-6 Trust in the Lord with all your heart and lean not to thy own understanding.* Here we see God asking us to Trust in Him with all our heart. This is something we have to do daily. The great part about it God will meet you where you are and daily you can grow in him. Then he tells us not to lean to our own understanding. This is great for the recovering person because it was your own understanding that got you into this problem. You were doing your best thinking and you ended up addicted to drugs/alcohol. It's time you "get from behind the wheel and let God do the driving".

The biggest problem for the Christian who becomes addicted to drugs or alcohol is there pride. Once they see that there is a problem they find it hard to ask for help in fear of what people might think and the embarrassment of their Church finding out is too great.

On the other hand, there are some practicing Christian addicts/alcoholics that continue to run to the Church for help. Deep down inside they know that God can deliver them. When and how is still a mystery? Even though they have been living in sin all week, they know deep down inside that their help comes from God. As their disease progresses they slowly disappear from Church. The guilt and remorse separates them from God and they hit a bottom quickly.

Step 3 for the recovering addict is a giant step. Anyone who decides to apply this step into his or her life will never regret it. Start by saying, "yes" to God, no matter what; and learning how to say "no" to the world.

Here at Step 3, we concentrate on giving God our whole day, everyday, "ONE DAY AT A TIME." We must set time aside everyday for the Lord, through prayer, meditation and reading God's Word. At Step 3, we have made up our minds to, not just be a hearer of God's Word, but a doer of God's Word. At Step 3, we begin to live as Christians (Christ-like).

Those who believe that this is a hard step are those who refuse to surrender to God totally. They believe they can skip this step and reap the benefits by working the rest of the steps. Those who choose to skip, or avoid, or leave Jesus out of their recovery, seem to go through life searching for victory. Even though they are free from drugs and alcohol, they continue to try and fill a void that can only be filled by Jesus. Peace, joy and love seem to elude them as they look for these things in all the wrong places. The recovering Christian individual has to make up his/her mind to live for God, or continue on this path of destruction; there is no in-between.

I have to admit, if there ever was a scripture that did not set well with me early in my Christian walk it was John 8:32, *"You shall know the truth and the truth shall make you free."* Working with Christian addicts and alcoholics, I began to question this scripture. How can you know the truth and be a junkie or an alcoholic? Some of the people who were coming to me for help have known the truth all their lives. Some grew up in Christian families, and understood this whole concept of Christianity or did they? Many could quote scripture from one cover of the Bible to the other. They knew the truth, but they could not stay free from drugs or alcohol. I actually avoided this scripture because I was meeting too many Christians bound to drugs and alcohol, I had no answer for them or myself.

Deep down in my heart I believed all the stories in the Bible were true; Jesus walking on water, God parting the Red Sea, or Jesus raising Lazarus from the dead. But I had a problem with *"You shall know the truth and the truth shall make you free."* After studying God's Word, I finally got my answer. The word *"know"* in this sentence means to *"live"* in the Greek translation (*Ginosko*). It is the recognition of truth by personal experience. Now this makes sense. You shall *"live"* the truth and the truth shall make you free. It is easy to see if anyone who lives the truth will be free. Many practicing addicts and alcoholic are not "living" the truth hanging around those old so-called friends. *"Do not be unequally yoked together with unbelievers. For what fellowship has righteousness with lawlessness? And what communion has light with darkness?"* (II Corinthians 6:14). It is impossible to live the truth spending weeknights in nightclubs, chasing the opposite sex, or justifying drinking a beer, etc. Some of us have developed deep-rooted habits that we think are "fun" and do not want to break them. Some of us hide behind the newness of being a Christian and not knowing the Word of God, but we all know right from wrong. The problem with Christian addicts/alcoholics is that they have made up there minds to live wrong. Living wrong is not an option for those who love the Lord. Living wrong separates us from God. Once we turn our backs on the truth, we enter into relapse territory.

If you find yourself not living the truth, understanding, and patience; asking God for forgiveness and repentance will be the key to our walk back to God's grace and mercy. It's as simple as one, two, three:
1. Patience – Not beating yourself up for being a babe in Christ and/or making mistakes.
2. Forgiveness – Forgiving yourself for mistakes and believing God has forgiven you.
3. Repentance – Learning to turn away from those things that God hates.

Everyone makes mistakes; no one is expected to be perfect. If you fall during this walk, God forbid, get up and ask for forgiveness and continue your walk. Get back up and continue doing what is right in the sight of the Lord.

Remember, Satan's job is to lure you back to him by any means necessary. He will use anything and everything possible to get you to return. Un-forgiveness, frustration, depression, and life's ups and downs have turned many recovering people away from God, and back to the old lifestyle.

Ephesians 6:13-14 Galatians 5:1 *Stand fast therefore in the liberty where with Christ has made you free, and be not entangled again in the yoke of bondage.* Going through the ups and down of life is a part of life that most addicts and alcoholics run from by using drugs and alcohol. With Christ on our side, we stand in our freedom knowing that God is able to bring us through; even when we were living in our sins, God was with us. As we grow in God we have to learn how to *"put on the full armor of God, so that when the day of evil comes, you maybe able to stand your ground, and after you have done everything, to stand. (14) Stand firm with the belt of truth buckled around your waist, with the breastplate of righteousness in place."* Here we clothe ourselves with the Word of God, renewing our minds and trusting God to fight our battles for us. Psalms 46:10 says, *"be still and know that I am God".* Sometimes we have to get out the way and watch God work. No matter what happens, we have to learn how to trust in God, and believe "everything is going to be all right."

I am convinced that if you accept Jesus Christ as your personal Lord and Savior, and believe in your heart that God raised Him from the dead, heaven is your home. If you make a quality decision to let God have complete control over your will and life, you can have heaven right here on earth. At the same time, there will be those who accept Christ into their lives, but still straddle the fence. They may make it into heaven, but they will have hell right here on earth. These will always wonder, what's wrong with them, why are they not succeeding? For the Christians, "GOD WILL NOT BLESS ANY MESS." If you decide to turn away or play games with the truth, God has many ways of getting your attention. Some addicts/alcoholics want to live a lukewarm lifestyle in Christ, then wonder why they are having so many problems. Revelations 3:16 explains, *"So, because you are lukewarm, neither hot nor cold, I am about to spit you out of my mouth."*

Making a quality decision means you spend quality time in prayer, and meditation, and studying God's Word and working on yourself. We must make a quality decision daily. Daily we must learn how to give our lives to God. This is a continued practice, until Jesus comes back.

In Luke 9:23 Jesus said, *"If anyone would come after me, he must deny himself and take up his cross daily and follow me."* (One day at a time.) Deny those things that you used to do, or still want to do and desire; give them to God and follow Him.

At Step 3, we are not asking you to walk on water, we are asking you to step out on faith and begin living right in the sight of God. We know this is new for most recovering people, so easy does it. Just like when you were out in the world and had separated yourself from God--God was still with you. How much more will God be with you now that you have turned your life over to Him?

Being sold out to God and allowing God to meet you where you are will be your life's goal. At Step 3, we have to make up are minds to be full-time Christians or to continue living the way we have been living. Making a conscience effort to live righteous, holy, and seeking God first is the action required in Step 3. Is it possible for you to be a 24/7 Christian?

At Step 3, we begin to recognize those people, places, and things that are not of God and a decision has to be made whether to keep them in our lives or discard them. When we begin to examine ourselves and are willing to get honest with ourselves there are some obvious people, places and things that we must separate ourselves from. Be aware that sometimes we unknowingly allow people, places and things into our lives and don't realize or deny that they are a problem. With the help of a sponsor and an honest look at our lives we are able to see that we have been worshiping people, places, and things; and that only God should have received that much time, and attention. Anything that we put before God becomes our god (mam-mon). We as recovering addicts/alcoholics worshipped the drugs we chose. We spent hours with it, money on it and when we didn't have it, we thought about it. Drugs and alcohol became our god. It is easy to see we worshipped drugs and alcohol, but now it is time to evaluate the lifestyle and the people, places, and things that went with it.

At Step 3 things change. If you are not willing to move to another level in Christ, return to the second Step, be honest with God, your sponsor or your counselor, and let them know that you are moving too fast. Most importantly, you have to be honest with yourself. God will meet you where you are, and He will love you until you are ready to love yourself and surrender all.

1. Define quality decision?

____

____

2. What is the difference between a quality decision and the relationship you had with the Lord in the past?

____

____

3. What is the difference between Savior and Lord?

____

____

4. What would it take for you to make that quality decision? What kind of changes would have to take place?

____

____

5. What must the recovering Christian make up his/her mind to do?

____

____

6. Explain John 8:32 and why it is important to the addict/alcoholic?

____

____

7. Explain Joshua 24:15.

____

____

8. Are you ready to be like Joshua? If so, why and how?

____

____

9. Anything you put before God is your god. List the gods you served before you arrived at Step 3.

____

____

10. This is an honest program, which god will you have a problem letting go of and why?

____

____

11. Explain, "God will not bless no mess".

____

____

12. Are you ready to make that quality decision?   Yes ☐   No   ☐

13. Explain your answer, and what would it take for you do be a full-time 24/7 Christian?

____

____

14. In your own words, summarize Step 3.

____

____

Step 4

Made a thorough and fearless moral examination of ourselves on paper
(2 Corinthians 13:5)

In order to carry out a successful fourth step, first you must fulfill a quality 3rd Step. In Step three, you learn to step out on faith, learning how to do things that you have never done. At Step 4, you have to step out on faith into an area that most addicts /alcoholics avoid because of fear. Satan will try to use fear to stop God's blessing for you here at Step 4. However, II Timothy 1:7-8 lets us know, *7For God gave us not a spirit of fearfulness; but of power and love and discipline. 8Be not ashamed therefore of the testimony of our Lord, nor of me his prisoner: but suffer hardship with the gospel according to the power of God..."* So in Christ we should fear nothing but God, and God is with us. We should not be ashamed of our past because God will use it for His glory. Here at Step 4 we turn and look right into our past and thank God for where he has brought us. The Bible also says at Philippians 4:13, *"I can do all things through Christ that strengthens me."* Those who trust in the Lord believe in the direction God is sending them. There is a reason God wants us to overcome the demons of our past. Conquering your past will launch you into your future.

We have found that those who have a hard time making a quality decision to let God have complete control over their will and life through His Word (Step #3), have a difficult time completing Step 4. Instead of trusting God, they would rather go back to Step 1 and start over.

Let's define the key words in the fourth step before we start.

1. Thorough - complete; extremely attentive to accuracy and detail; painstaking. Here we leave out nothing, taking our time to look under every rock with a magnifying glass.
2. Fearless - without regard of consequences; bold. Here we trust in the Word of God believing everything things going to be all right.
3. Moral - conforming to accepted or established principles of right conduct; upright; virtuous; honest. A proper and honest account of our lives is needed here. This is not a race so take your time.
4. Examination: -- inspection; inquiry; investigation. Medically speaking -- to evaluate general health or determine the cause of illness. Examine your motives, what really happened?

Most people in recovery and even people not in recovery ask this question, why a Step 4? Why do I have to bring up something that is filled with pain? This is asked by 95% of all addicts/alcoholics that ever walked through the doors of recovery. Some are hesitant to do it because they are afraid of what they might find. Others can't figure out the point of the exercise; so since they can't figure it out (with their sick thinking) on their own, why do it? And others are just plain lazy and they think it's too much work for them to do.

Some even sabotage their recovery, they subconsciously find a reason to get high or drink so they can start over. Others fight with all their might when they get to the fourth Step. They have an idea what their past looks like, so out of fear they stop this process.

Christian addicts/alcoholics in defiance of this step will use scripture such as II Corinthians 5:17, *"Therefore, if anyone is in Christ he is a new creation; old things have passed away and behold all things become new."* Their argument is, if they are "new," why do they have to go back in their past?

What Paul was saying in II Corinthians 5:17 is, yes you are a new creation, but new in your spirit. When we walk through the doors of the Church, our flesh, our thinking, our behavior, is still the same. When you walk through the doors of the Church, your bad thinking and bad habits walk through the doors with you. Your spirit has surrendered to God but it will take time for you to be totally new in your flesh. Take an honest look at yourself, examine yourself, and find out who you really are. The fourth step is designed to reveal some of those fleshly behaviors that will hinder our walk with God. Another scripture that is always used by Christian that are afraid to conquer there past is Philippians 3:13b, *"but this thing I do, forgetting those things, which are behind, and reaching forth unto those things which are before."* Yes, we believe you have to forget those old things in your past, but first you have to identify some of these things that have been covered up and will continue to haunt you in your future. Addicts and alcoholics are experts at stuffing or covering up devastating events from their past. Deep-rooted things, which cause them to be defensive, always protecting what little pride, they have left. Because of what they remember they become standoffish or loners living in their own world justifying their every action and why they live and act the way they do.

For years, addicts and alcoholics have been running from these haunting memories, never wanting to face the pain that changed their lives. Every time these memories rear their ugly heads, we medicate ourselves with the alcohol or the drug of our choice, or the sin of our choice (sex, illegal activities); never knowing why we have returned to the drugs, alcohol, or behavior that always gets us into trouble.

The Bible talks about a man who was just like the addicts and alcoholics of today. This man lived in the graveyard until Jesus came to him and changed his life. Mark 5: 1-15 *"Then they came to the other side of the sea, to the country of the Gadarenes (2) And when He had come out of the boat, immediately there met Him out of the tombs a man with an unclean spirit (3) who had his dwelling among the tombs; and no one could bind him not even with chains, (4) because he had often been bound with shackles and chains. And the chains had been pulled apart by him, and the shackles broken in pieces; neither could anyone tame him. (5) And always, night and day, he was in the mountains and in the tombs, crying out and cutting himself with stones. (6) When he saw Jesus from afar, he ran and worshiped Him. (7) And he cried out with a loud voice and said, "What have I to do with You, Jesus, Son of the Most High God? I implore you by God that You do not torment me." (8) For He said to him, "Come out of the man, unclean spirit!" (9) Then He asked him, "What is your name?" And he answered, saying "My name is Legion: for we are many." (10) Also he begged Him earnestly that He would not send them out of the country. (11) Now a large herd of swine was feeding there near the mountains. (12) So all the demons begged Him, saying, "Send us to the swine, that we may enter them." (13) And at once Jesus gave them permission. Then the unclean spirits went out and entered the swine (there were about three thousand); and the herd ran violently down the steep place into the sea, and drowned in the sea. (14) So those who fed the swine fled and they told it in the city and in the country. And they went out to see what it was that had happened (15) Then they came to Jesus and saw the one who had been demon-possessed and had the legion, sitting and clothed and in his right mind. And they were afraid."*

First think about what this guy must have went through. How he was treated by the towns people. No friends or family to support him all alone living in a cemetery, separated from his family because of these demons living inside him. Today he would have been diagnosed with a mental condition. Haunted by memories of hurtful people trying to subdue him with chains, cutting himself with stones trying to end his life.

Jesus meets this man where he is. If addicts and alcoholics take a good look back on their lives and get honest they will see where God met them while they where at their lowest point, somewhere in a dope house using and abusing drugs or alcohol. Most of the time it comes during a low point in their lives, God shows up through a concerned loved one or a friend or stranger, telling them about the goodness of God and how they should surrender to God's love.

The second similarity is in verse two; this brother lived in the tombs. In every city in America, addicts and alcoholic live and die in the graveyards of their mind. They walk around like zombies searching for another hit or fix in a desperate attempt to drown out the painful mistakes made in their past.

The third similarity is in verses three and four, the town in which he lived tried everything in their power to stop this brother but nothing worked. He broke the chains that were put on him. Everyday someone is coming up with another way to treat the suffering addict/alcoholic and it seems like the problem is only getting worse.

At verse nine, Jesus asked the demon what is your name and the demon said, "My name is legion, for we are many." In recovery, we have to confront the demons that reside in a person's mind and haunt them daily. The baby that was aborted, the money that you stole from your parents, the demoralizing things you did to get the drugs or while you were under the influence, and so on, and so on. This brother had over two thousand demons living inside him and the Bible called them legion. The definition of Legion –: in ancient Rome was an army division of 2,000 to 6,000 soldiers, including the Calvary. We minister to addicts and alcoholics that are consumed with demons called legions and they live in the memories of their mind.

In verse fifteen, after Jesus gave the demons the permission to go into a herd of swine and they violently ran off a cliff, the town's people came out to see what happen, (but really they were upset because they had just lost a lot of money in losing those pigs) and the Bible says they found the once demon possessed man clothed and in his right <u>mind.</u> Sanity returned when God freed his mind.

We find that the fourth Step is not only spiritually sound but clinically sound as well. Psychologists tell us that we, as people, hold on to or cover up too many things that have happened in our past. Events in our lives that we try to suppress, hoping they will one day go away. If we do not release them in a positive manner, they begin to build up like a boiling pressure cooker. This pressure cooker can explode at any time, sometimes over the smallest thing. Once this happens, an addict/alcoholic will return to what is easy for them, using drugs or alcohol in an attempt to medicate the pain.

If we had this brother in Mark 5 conduct a 4th step I wonder what would it say? How long would his resentment list be? How many on this list would be family members and love ones. The 4th step teaches you to uncover those deep dark secrets that can come back and terrorize you when you least expect it.

Deep-rooted memories such as rape, child molestation, and child neglect, the loss of a loved one, or even issues of abandonment if not dealt with properly will constantly haunt the recovering addict/alcoholic. Satan's job is to magnify these memories in that person's life when everything is going well. Sometimes triggers are not that clear and recognizable. They can be many small events or not so noticeable behaviors. Innocent things that you would never consider as being the reason why a person returned to drinking or using can be the trigger that caused them to use. A talk show on finding your long lost father is a trigger for someone who has no father, or never had a good relationship with his/her father. Being around a person with kids is a trigger for someone who found out they cannot have kids. Someone raising their voice is a trigger to someone who came from of an abusive family. These things are brought out and faced in a 4th Step, if you are honest, fearless, and thorough.

Some try to stuff feelings only to have them surface years later. Some drink and use drugs; others overeat, and still others work all the time in an attempt to stay busy to avoid their past. As their past begins to catch up with them, and Satan floods their minds with the things they did or things that happened to them, some commit suicide as a way of escape.

We know that it is impossible to run from ourselves. One writer wrote, "everywhere you go, there you are." For a recovering addict/alcoholic this attempt to escape from their past is especially dangerous. Without any apparent reason, an addict/alcoholic will go out and practice his or her disease. When asked why, after years of being free from drugs or alcohol, the addict/alcoholic will tell you "I just don't know why." Ironically, they really don't know. They don't understand this disease is alive and well inside them. They don't know that something in their past is tearing at their future and causing them to drink or get high. This may be the only honest thing they have said in a long time, I just don't know. Truthfully, they really don't know why they returned to drinking and using.

It is vital that the recovering person completes a thorough fourth Step. You may not see it now, but the freedom you will experience will make your walk with Christ a joyful walk. You will be able to move freely in Christ and in your day-to-day walk. You will not be afraid of your past, and you will not allow it to effect your future.

There are several reasons we specifically ask you to write down these things on paper.

    1.   You cannot rely on your memory in detail when dealing with your past. Once they are on paper we learn to confront our past and learn how to put it behind us forever.

    2.   We also found that there is a release and an escape like no other in writing a thorough and fearless moral examination on paper. Once you see it in black and white, it takes the sting out of what happen.

How do you write a 4th Step? Where do you start? Do I write about my family or myself? These are some of the questions we are asked by recovering people who arrive at the fourth Step.

Here are several different ways to actually write a 4th Step. First, it is very important that you write a 4th Step with someone who has been through the process and has written a 4th Step. This person cannot be your Pastor or a good friend. This person has to be working the process of recovery in his or her own life.

This person should be someone that you trust, someone who will not co-sign your excuses or look down on you because of your past. This person should also be someone that will not join in your pity-party, they should always direct you back to recovery. If you share what you are going through with someone who does not understand the disease of addiction, or who does not understand the process of recovery, that person could make you feel worse than you felt before you began this fourth Step.

One way to write a 4th Step is to just sit down and start writing your life history, noting the good with the bad as far back as you can remember. Take each member of your family and write as much as you can on each family member and your relationship with him or her. It must be in-depth, detailed, and thorough. You must write down, if you like him, if you love him, if you dislike him or hate him and WHY. If you do not address the why, you are wasting your time. When writing a 4th Step, you do not have to finish it in one sitting. Most sponsors will guide you through each family member, or each situation, until you are finished. (Remember, you must finish.)

This step only becomes difficult if you have not surrendered yourself in the third Step. Those that have no problem in diving into this fourth step made a quality decision to let God have complete control over their will and life (3rd Step). They believe and know that God is ordering their steps so they live in the safety of God's bosom. These recovering addicts/alcoholics are willing to go anywhere because they know God would never leave them, nor forsake them; even when they allow God to lead them into their past and dig up those things that have kept them bound. *"Ye though I walk through the valley of the shadow of death I will fear no evil for you are with me; Your rod and your staff, they comfort me."* (Psalms 23:4). Those that believe have no fear of the fourth Step.

Then you have those that fear the fourth Step. They are afraid to go down some of those dark painful paths. This group has to look at their relationship with God and how much they really believe that God will do what He said He would do!

Step 4 will reveal hidden sides of our nature that over the years have become dysfunctional. Hidden in the shrubbery of our behavior, protected by the high fence of denial, lies, resentment, anger, frustration and despair; they have lived with us so long they become an accepted part of our life. Most of these issues go unnoticed, so they go unresolved by the individual. The issues that are noticed seem impossible to change, or the individual's fear of change keeps them from addressing the situation. Others only see the affects of addiction and never face the cause. They understand that they have a bad attitude and they are willing to work on bettering the attitude, but they never attack the core of the problem or what birthed this negative attitude in the first place.

When approaching the fourth Step remembers, being thorough, detailed, complete and in-depth is the key to a successful fourth Step. Take your time being precise and reaching as far back into your past as you possibly can.

Be not afraid of confronting the good and the bad things that happened in your childhood. Events changed your way of thinking and altered your perception of life making you the person you are today. Examples: A family member rapes a girl at a very young age, and for years, she never tells anyone. When she becomes a woman she has problems giving herself to the man she falls in love with. So, she drinks and uses because of another failed relationship. A boy was abandoned by his father, and for years, he longed for a relationship with him. Now that he is a man, he has a hard time bonding with his own son. He is unable to fill the void inside that is causing him to be emotionally distant.

In this fourth Step, you are on a fact-finding mission. Your past plays an important part in who you are, and why you act the way you do. A disobedient lifestyle led you to drugs and alcohol; it is your past that keeps you stuck in the muck and the mire.

1. How will you know you are ready to attack the fourth Step?

____

____

2. What is the purpose of this fourth Step?

____

____

3. Do you have "fears" about uncovering your past?   ☐ Yes   ☐ No

4. If yes, what are they?

____

____

5. Define resentment.

____

____

6. If faith and trust are "action words," how will you apply them here at the fourth Step?

____

____

____

RESENTMENT LIST

(Circle one answer for each person.)

Wife	Yes	No	Husband	Yes	No
Mother	Yes	No	Father	Yes	No
Sister	Yes	No	Brother	Yes	No
Children	Yes	No	Self	Yes	No
Grandmothers	Yes	No	Grandfathers	Yes	No
Aunts	Yes	No	Uncles	Yes	No
Cousin	Yes	No	Friends	Yes	No
Employees	Yes	No	Bosses	Yes	No
Co-Workers	Yes	No	Business Partners	Yes	No
Police	Yes	No	Judges	Yes	No
Teachers	Yes	No	Classmates	Yes	No
Lawyers	Yes	No	Preachers	Yes	No
God	Yes	No	Counselors	Yes	No
Boy Friend	Yes	No	Girl Friend	Yes	No

If there is anyone else that you can think of, please list.

____

____

In answering these next questions, we suggest you share your answers with your sponsor or counselor. They will be able to assist and encourage you as you go.

7. On a separate sheet of paper, list those people that you resent, from the most resented to the least resented. (Write each person on separate sheets of paper.)

8. On another sheet list, why do you resent them? (Explain fully.)

9. Then on another sheet, list what part did you to play in the destruction of this relationship? (Only your part – this takes a lot of honesty and focus.)

10. Can you forgive each person?   Yes ☐   No ☐

11. If no, "Why"?

____

____

12. For all the wrongs you committed, do you want God to forgive you? Yes ☐ No ☐

13. Answer #9 again. Can you forgive each person on your resentment list?
       Yes ☐   No ☐

14. Get down on your knees and pray a loving prayer for each person that you have resentment against. Remember God brought you this far; are you willing to past the test? God is waiting.

THE DEFINITION
OF
FORGIVENESS IS:
ACTING AS IF IT NEVER HAPPENED!

Step 5

Confessed to God in the name of Jesus, admitted to ourselves, and unashamedly admit the exact nature of our wrongs to another human being. (Proverbs 28:13, James 5:16, 1 John 1:9)

It is no accident that after you have written down all these things in your fourth Step, after you have faced all your fears and resentments, and after you have written down all these demoralizing details on paper, here at Step 5 you must confess to God and to another human being the exact nature of _**your**_ wrongs.

However, before you attempt to attack this step you have to know how to come to God. This step starts by saying "Confess to God in the name of Jesus." Why do we come in the name of Jesus? The most famous prayer ever said by most addicts/alcoholics is, "God will you please help me." Especially after drinking and using for weeks at a time and after destroying everything and everyone that gets in our way. We turned to God tired of getting high, tired of not being high, tired of being up all night, and tired of seeing the sun come up in the morning--just tired of being tired. Finally we hit a mental, physical, and spiritual bottom and we cried out "God will you please help me." God, because of His grace and His love for us, answered our prayers and came to our rescue. It is something about crying out to God with a sincere heart that gets God's attention.

I have discovered many recovering people (this writer included) coming into the Church not knowing that God has made it very plain and simple how we are supposed to come to Him in prayer. John 14:6 says, _"Jesus answered, "I am the way and the truth and the life. No one comes to the Father but by me."_ The recovering person must understand that God sent Jesus here to be mediator between Almighty God and us. Therefore, the proper way to approach God is through his Son, Jesus Christ. "In Jesus' name" should be the beginning and the ending of our prayers.

Next, we have to examine this word unashamedly: not ashamed, without guilt or embarrassment, without doubt. Guilt is a powerful tool that Satan uses to keep us from growing and getting all we can from God. There are many reasons why we unashamedly admit to another human being. Let's take a look at a few:

1. We know that God loves us and that He has forgiven us.
2. Therefore, we can keep our heads up high because we know where we were before God rescued us.
3. One day you will find that your past will help someone else.

The next part of Step 5 is one of the most important concepts in recovery, confession. For many practicing addicts/alcoholics (this writer included) going to God wasn't that difficult, but telling someone else the ups and downs of what went on in our life is not easy to do. Exposing our secret life that no one knows about; the things that we promised ourselves we would take to our graves. When I first wrote these things down on paper, I guarded that paper with my life! Why share these things with another human being?

The answer is simple. God will begin to deal with that self-righteous spirit that dwells in every recovering person. By the time most recovering addicts/alcoholics arrive at Step

5, they know that drugs and alcohol is only the symptom of a greater problem. At Step 5, we come face-to-face with the cause. Some recovering addicts/alcoholics avoid this step, and some of them return to using because they avoided what got them there in the first place.

"Confessed to God and to another human being." First, we have to believe that God has forgiven us of all our sins. Once we have given all those pains, all those hurtful events to God, next we have to be obedient to the Word of God and share these events with another human being.

We have already learned at Step 2 how to turn it over to God. We know that recovering people beat themselves up more than anyone on this planet could ever do. More than our mothers, more than our fathers, more than our loved ones and friends. We find a secret place and cry until there are no more tears; never letting anyone know the pain we are suffering.

Even though you have finished your fourth step, Satan's job is to test your faith. Are you really ready to face your old life and deal with the pain? Do you really believe God has forgiven you for some of the things in your past? Psalms 103:12 *says, "as far as the East is from the West, so far has he removed our transgressions from us."* The Bible also says at Romans 4:7, *"Blessed are they whose transgressions are forgiven, whose sins are covered. Blessed is the man whose sins the Lord will never count against him."* Here God's Word consoles us. All those negative things we did in the past have been forgiven and will not be held against us. To this day, many addicts and alcoholics have a hard time surrendering to God because Satan holds them in a state of un-forgiveness. He dangles all the things they did in the past and does his best to convince them that they are not worthy of God's goodness. When we begin to forgive ourselves, Satan's job is to remind us of our past. When we give that life to God, we have to learn to walk in His forgiveness. God's Word says *He will never count it against us* and as long as you don't bring that part of your life up, God won't either.   Here at step 5, we share this part of our life with our sponsor (see Chapter II "Why a Sponsor") who will continue to remind you of God's love for you and that you have been forgiven.

We must unashamedly admit the exact nature of our wrongs to another human being. *"Confess your faults one to another, and pray one for another, that ye may be healed. The effectual fervent prayer of a righteous man availeth much."* (James 5:16) Every psychologist in the field of counseling today uses this verse of the Bible, even though secular psychologists will never admit it. Once you walk into a psychologist's office the first thing he/she will have you do is sit or lie down, and talk about what is going on with you. As you get comfortable and begin to feel safe in his presence, his job is to get you to open up concerning your faults. In James 5:16, after we have *confessed one to another* God is asking us to also *pray for one another that you may be healed* (this is something that most psychologists will not do). Healed from what? Healed from the pressures of life, that seems to pull us down daily. Healed from the wrong decisions, we make daily and have made in our lifetime. Healed from the guilt that we carry around, but try to hide, and healed from our past that continues to haunt us.   This is a perfect example of God working through other people.

Once we start sharing and praying with other people, they can stand in agreement with us as we walk this road of recovery. Satan's job is to remind us of our past sins. He wants to trick us into believing that we are not worthy of being free, or of being Christians.

Our sponsors or our friends that we have shared Step 4 with, can remind us that we have already confessed these sins to God, so why are we still carrying these sins around?

Bishop Charles E. Blake of West Angeles Church of God in Christ, shares a story about a man who knelt down at the altar for prayer. As the 'man of God' prayed for everyone at the altar and told them to cast all their cares upon God, for 'He cares for you'. the man on his knees knew that the 'man of God' was talking to him. When the 'man of God' finished the prayer, everyone kneeling at the altar arose and headed back to their seats. Suddenly the man who had been on his knees turned around went back to the altar, picked up all those care, and burdens that he had left, and returned to his seat. This is a classic example of an addict/alcoholic having a hard time forgiving himself or herself and letting go.

By the time an addict and alcoholic enters recovery they have burned most of their bridges and isolated themselves from friends and family. Most are carrying the weight of the world on their shoulders and continue to use to medicate the pain. Even in recovery, many continue this silence concerning their problems because they refuse to participate in fourth and the fifth Step.

Stacking their problems on top of each other is like waiting for a pressure cooker to blow its top. When an addict/alcoholic compiles his/her deep secrets without releasing them in a healthy manner, the recovering person is bound to explode one-day. Most of the time this explosion returns the recovering person back to what they know best-- drinking and using.

At Step 5, we are taught to release these growth-stunting secrets in a healthy manner with people that care about our well-being. Once these secrets are released from the dungeons of our minds, prayer plays an important part in keeping them locked out. Prayer and talking to our sponsors help us to keep that secret before God and not take it back to the dungeons of our mind and soul. Once this is done God does the rest, and healing begins to take place. Slowly the secret loses its power and we find ourselves sharing with others that same secret that we swore we would never tell and about the freedom we now have. That same secret we pledged to "take to the grave" is now a testimony shared with others who are facing the same fears.

At one time, I used to ask the question why, "why did God allow me to go through such pains as a kid or as young adults and even adults." Today I know that God allowed me to go through these different situations knowing that He would one day get the glory, and in His time, He would heal or deliver me from each situation. Now it is my job to tell the story of how I got over. (Giving God the Glory!)

For the person just arriving at Step 5, this is hard to see and that is why a person should not attempt this step alone. This is why a sponsor is important, someone that has walked through this step and knows the fears you will face (see Chapter II "Why a Sponsor").

Confessing our faults/sins every night before the Father is something we must do before our heads hit the pillow. As you grow, you will learn to confess all during the day. And never forget, to end every prayer **"IN JESUS' NAME."**

1. Explain John 14:6.

____

____

____

2. In your own words, why do you think God set it up this way?

____

____

____

3. What is the purpose of confession?

____

____

4. What do you fear most about sharing your fourth Step with another human being?

____

____

5. If God has forgiven you, why do you have a hard time forgiving yourself?

____

____

6. What is the reason for sharing your fourth Step to another human being?

____

____

7. What kind of person will you look for to share your fourth Step with?

____

8. Have you chosen someone? Yes ☐   No ☐   If not why? If so, who?

____

____

9. Now that you have shared this information how do you feel? (There is no wrong answer.)

____

____

10. Why do we continue to pray about something you have given to God?

____

____

11. Are you willing to move on?   Yes ☐   No ☐

12. How will you do it?

____

____

*Happiness comes from within

and is found in the present

moment by making peace with

your past and looking forward

to your future*

Step 6

Became entirely ready to have God take away all these blocks to our freedom in Christ. (Galatians 5:1, Hebrews 12: 1, 2, Psalms 86:10-13, Psalms 119:57-59)

Once you have finished your fourth and fifth step, the picture of the real you will become clearer.   With the help of your God, sponsor, and/or concerned Christian friends, you will begin to identify critical thinking errors, inappropriate addicted behaviors, and character defects that you have adopted as a result of a drinking and/or using lifestyle.

Step 6 prepares us for taking an honest look at who we have become. This step lets us know that by accepting Christ through the process of recovery we can now honestly look at the parts of ourselves that we don't like. We call these behaviors character defects. Defects of character stem from the sin that every man is born with. The grandfather of all sin is Pride. Pride is the reason Satan and all his angels was kicked out of Heaven. When you look at the list of character defects at the end of this chapter you will see that all character defects link to or they connected to others. For instance arrogance, links with conceit, self important, vanity, aggressiveness, along with others. This is why the bible says at *Luke 11:24 – 26 24"When the unclean spirit goes out of a man, it passes through waterless places seeking rest, and not finding any, it says, 'I will return to my house from which I came.' 25"And when it comes, it finds it swept and put in order. 26"Then it goes and takes along seven other spirits more evil than itself, and they go in and live there; and the last state of that man becomes worse than the first."*

The lifestyle of the addict/alcoholic is filled with evil, demonic spirits. Nothing good comes from it. When people get trap in that way of life many of these character defects attach to the person. Some are there as defense mechanisms used to protect that person in a evil world.   Often character defects are behaviors which allowed us to survive the difficult environments we experienced as children coming from dysfunctional families.

Letting go of character defects can, therefore, feel like a threat to our survival and in no way or means will it be easy to accomplish. Some call this major surgery because it affects every aspect of your life. It changes the way you see yourself and other people. The Bible says at Ezekiel 11:19, *"I will remove from them their heart of stone and give them a heart of flesh."* Most addicts walk through the doors of recovery with a "chip on their shoulders. They can always find the blame in other people but have a hard time seeing what part they played in any negative situation. They find it easy to blame others and always think that they are not far from normal thinking.

Are you brave enough to ask the question "Who is the real <u>(your name here)</u>?" Most people who attempt to answer this question have a hard time finding an answer. Because of defense mechanism put into place due to past hurts and surviving the environment in which we live, we have no clue of who we really are. At this point in our lives, some of us are incapable of being honest with ourselves to tell the truth once we get a glimpse of what we have become.

For those who are brave enough to become "entirely ready," by taking these findings to God and humbly surrender to the change that is about to take place, grow by leaps and bounds. They realize that this type of change can only come from God himself. *Jeremiah, 18:3-6 "Then I went down to the potter's house, and there he was making something at the wheel. (4) And the vessel that he made of clay was marred in the hand of the potter; so he made it again into another vessel, as it seemed good to the potter to make. (5)Then the word of the Lord came to me, saying: (6)O house of Israel can I not do with you as this potter? Says the Lord "Look as the clay is in the potter's hand so are you in My hand O House of Israel."* God is saying that because He loves you He has the right to change you and make you into what he wants you to be. At the sixth step you prepare yourself to be stripped of all old behaviors and becoming a whole new being.

Some may argue that drugs and alcohol are the root cause of other problems and once the addict stops drinking and using the problem is solved. You may have never robbed, stolen, lied, or cheated anyone while in your addiction, but in God's eyes you were wrong and His eyes are the only ones that count. If you failed to be the husband, wife, mother, father, sister, brother or friend that you were supposed to be, then you cheated those that deserved better. Many active addicts say things like "I'm not hurting anyone but myself." These statements are not only selfish but also ungodly.

Even though you have begun your process of recovery, accepted Christ as your Savior and revealed those deep dark secrets, a lot of work still has to be done. While immersed in the drug culture, some inappropriate coping skills or 'bad habits" began to develop. Some of these habits helped us make it through some very hard times. For instance, being very defensive protected us from mean and evil people, but in this new life, we have to learn how to trust people, and trust in God. There is absolutely no use for a bad attitude in this new life in Christ. When we accepted Christ into our lives, negative behaviors like having a bad attitude came into the kingdom with us. If only one bad habit came into the kingdom with you, you're batting a thousand. Lying, cheating, deceiving, backbiting, and jealousy are just a few behaviors that we unknowingly walk through the doors of the Church with. We have to remember that the Church is a big spiritual hospital where sick people come to get well. We also have to remember that alcoholics/addicts are sicker than most.

When we crossed over from darkness into His marvelous light, we brought most of our defects of character, if not all of our garbage, with us. Some of these character defects have been a part of us so long that they have become spirits. Things like disobedience, resentment, anger, laziness, lying, un-forgiveness, gossiping, backbiting; all motivated by pride and selfishness and block our freedom in Christ.

As we slowly begin to take steps in the Lord, we should always be striving to be the best person in Christ that we can be. The Bible says in *Philippians 3:14, "I press toward the mark for the prize of the high calling of God in Christ Jesus."* We know that some of our character defects can hinder our walk with the Lord, especially when God has revealed them.

For the addict/alcoholic, a change in our behavior is a must because without change, recovery is impossible. You must change people, change places, and changes things that you associate with to be successful. At Step 6, we must become "entirely ready" or be willing to take an honest look our character defects. Achieving change requires commitment and dedication to the recovery process and our spiritual walk. If we are unsuccessful, we will find ourselves in the same place in our sobriety; always wondering why everybody around us is growing spiritually and we are not. This will bring out other faults such as jealousy and bitterness. Once again, Satan has managed to take our eyes off the Lord and we find ourselves going backwards instead of higher in God.

Psalms 51:10 *states "Create in me a clean heart, Oh God; and renew a right spirit within me."* This is a great prayer to remember as we grow and walk in the Lord. As you renew the heart, the rest of the body follows, but this doesn't happen overnight. The Bible also says in Proverbs 4:23 *above all else, guard your heart, for it is the wellspring of life.* Satan's job is to change your way of thinking by urging you to adopt character defects as a way of life. Other live in denial never recognizing that he or she have a problem. "What is there to fix if nothings broke". Here again many recovering addicts/alcoholics concentrate on the drugs and alcohol and not the root of the problem. They believe they are "bad people trying to be good instead of sick people trying to get well." This is the reason we examine ourselves daily, making sure we stay focused on our sickness and are not led astray. Recovery teaches us that something is broken inside us, something that can be fixed by the power of God.

Remember this change will not come overnight so "Easy Does It," but "Do It." We thank God that He does not reveal all our defects of character to us at once. That would be unfair, and most recovering people would not be able to handle a complete overhaul overnight. God gives us one, two, maybe three defects at a time because trying to correct all these defects would be too great a challenge. Most would give up all together, believing this is an impossible task. This is another reason why it is okay to be a babe in Christ and why we should take our time as a babe. Revealing everything at once could leave most of us worse off than when we started. (*Remember God will not give no more than you can handle.*) So, if God reveals this character defect to you, it is your responsibility to face it, get totally honest with it, pray about it and be willing to change it.

At Step 6, God is not finished with you yet. As a matter of fact, we have a long way to go. We, as recovering people who have been rescued by God almighty, should want to do our best to please God by living righteous and holy. Working on ourselves will be something that we will have to continue to do until Jesus comes back.

Becoming "willing" will be the hardest part of this step. Accepting the fact that you've been living with this defect is not easy to accept. Some defects become a part of our personality and we do our best to justify our behavior. Therefore, we depend on our sponsor, Christian friends, counselors, our peers and the Word of God to lovingly show us our faults. But even listening to someone else can sometime be hard, especially when your defect of character happens to be lack of trust or anger. Lack of trust makes it hard to listen and to believe the information you receive is correct. Those with anger issues take constructive criticism personally, lashing out at anyone trying to help them. Finding someone to trust and listen to will be their biggest obstacle.

When the real you shows up, your flaws show up with you, and for the counselor and the recovering addict/alcoholic this can sometimes be overwhelming. It's very easy to point out defects of character when a person is open, honest, not holding back and showing everyone around them who they really are. They wear everything on their sleeve.

Then there is the quiet individual. This person never reveals to others who they really are. This group will build a wall around themselves only letting a selected few enter, if any. They are professionals at flying under the smoke screen and do their best at not being noticed. In a rehab, they make no waves and break no rules.

Then there is the individual who is like a chameleon; they can become whatever you want them to be. If a group is acting a particular way, they learn how to fit right in, and if this group or individual is acting another way, no problem they change and learn how to fit in there. If the fashionable thing is joining Church, they join Church. They learn how and when to say "Amen", they sing in the choir, and memorize a few scriptures. A recovering addict/alcoholic that lives like a chameleon and brings that type of behavior into this new life only hinders the recovery process because it takes longer for this person to begin the needed work. Rarely does a person with this behavior succeed in recovery because they change so much they don't know who they are. If a person never "gets real" with his or herself, what will they work on? Identify those blocks to your freedom, name them and become willing to let God take them away.

Surrender throw up the white flag, stop trying to be this <u>good</u> person on your own. (We're not bad people trying to be good; we're sick people trying to get well.) God is ready to do a work in you that will be pleasing to Him and He will get the glory. We remember a saying "When there's no change, there's no change." This is a very simple statement but right to the point. There must be a change in our behavior so we can move in the will of God. Are you ready to change? Are you ready to let God take away all these blocks to your freedom in Christ?

Character Defects The Secret Sin

1.) Self-importance   2.) Rebellious   3.) Hopeless   4.) Victim   5.) Judgmental

6.) Fear   7.) Unrealistic goals   8.) Critical   9.) Negativity   10.) Jealousy

11.) Insecurity   12.) Needy   13.) Greed   14.) Lust   15.) Resentful

16.) Anger   17.) Self-hatred   18.) Abusive   19.) Prejudice   20.) Hatred

21.) Self-righteous   22.) Easily frustrated   23.) Envy   24.) Denial   25.) Control

26.) Manipulation   27.) Dishonesty   28.) Morbid   29.) Self-pity   30.) Rigid

31.) Never satisfied   32.) Inconsistent   33.) Pride   34.) Nosiness   35.) Guilt

36.) Close-minded   37.) Demanding   38.) Selfish   39.) Shame   40.) Arrogant

41.) Materialistic   42.) Self centered   43.) Alienated   44.) Gossip   45.) Gluttony

46.) Not supportive   47.) Unforgiving   48.) Sarcastic   49.) Passive   50.) Meanness

51.) Over analytical   52.) Conditional   53.) Sabotaging   54.) Standoffish   55.) Depressed

56.) Self sufficient   57.) Competitive   58.) Egotistical   59.) Extremist   60.) Aggressive

61.) Complaining   62.) Codependent   63.) Betraying   64.) Dramatic   65.) Obsessive

66.) Procrastination   67.) Inconsiderate   68.) Intolerant   69.) Laziness   70.) Slyness

71.) Dishonorable   72.) Rationalizing   73.) Vengeful   74.) Doubtful   75.) Rejecting

76.) Disconnected   77.) Grandstanding   78.) Rumination   79.) Insensitive   80.) Escapism

81.) Pessimism   82.) Unwillingness   83.) Justification   84.) Paranoid   85.) Destructive

86.) Dependent   87.) Defensive   88.) Violent   89.) Easily overwhelmed

90.) Fantasy/ magical thinking   91.) Compulsive   92.) Perfection   93.) Conceited

94.) Vain   95) Strict   96) Enabler   97) Obsessive

98) People pleasing   99) Narrow-minded   100) Mean

1. "Who is the real <u>(your name)?"</u> Honestly explain who you are on paper. (Hint: What kind of job you have is not who you are.)

____

____

2. What type of character "defects" can become spirits?

____

____

2. Which ones do you see in your life?

____

3. Are you willing to take a look at some of these defects of character in your life?

Yes ☐   No ☐

4. Are you willing to let someone point a few defects of character out to you?

Yes ☐   No ☐

5. Who would that person(s) be? (It could also be a group of people)

____

6. What character defects came in with you when you walked through the doors of the Church, started recovery, or rededicated your life to Christ?

____

____

7. In your own words, explain Step 6?

____

____

8. How will you become ready to change these defects of character?

____

____

Step 7

Humbly asked God in the name of Jesus and thanked Him for His mercy and for giving us the strength to overcome our faults. (John 16:24, 1 Peter 5: 6-10, James 4:10, Psalms 51:10, Psalms 19:12-14)

In Step 6 we acknowledge our faults and accept the fact that they exist in our lives. We take a real good look at how they have affected our lives and the people around us. Here at Step 7, we look for positive ways to rid ourselves of these behaviors that keep us from growing in God. After recognizing your faults, it is now time for you do something about them. Yes all of them.

As we *"press toward the mark for the prize of the high calling of God in Christ Jesus."* God will "with all his wisdom" put things before you that is displeasing in his sight, stunts your growth, prevents you from being the person God wants you to be. At Step 7 it's time to take action!

The first word in this passage is **humble**. (Humble - not proud or haughty, in behavior, attitude, or spirit; no stuck on self, I or me.) This is one of the most powerful words in the Bible, and for recovering people one of the hardest behaviors to acquire. But it is one of the key offensive tools needed to make this change. If we take a look at this word "humble," we will learn that it is the opposite of "pride". Pride is the grandfather of most defects of character known to man. Pride is what urges the addict or alcoholic to take that first drink or hit. Pride keeps an addict or alcoholic drinking and using as long as they do. It was pride that got Satan kicked out of heaven! *"Because he exalted himself, he was doomed to the lowest hell"* (Isaiah 14:12-15). The direct opposite of Satan's behavior was Jesus humbling Himself at the cross and laying down His life for us. All through the Word of God, great men of God humbled themselves, and because of their humility, God blessed their lives and their situations.

While we were in our disease, we were caught up in pride. Even though the warning signs were all around, we did what we wanted to do. Most of us knew right from wrong, but we did wrong. Humility plays a big part in our recovery. Learning how to humble ourselves will be a life-long task.

I Peter 5:6-10"Humble yourselves therefore, under God's mighty hand, that he may lift you up in due time. (7)Cast all your anxiety on him because he cares for you. (8)Be self-controlled and alert. Your enemy the devil prowls around like a roaring lion looking for someone to devour. (9)Resist him, standing firm in the faith, because you know that your brothers throughout the world are undergoing the same kind of sufferings. (10)and the God of all grace, who called you to his eternal glory in Christ, after you have suffered a little while, will himself restore you and make you strong, firm and steadfast.". Learning how to humble yourself when everything inside you is saying, "these are *my* friends and I can hang around anyone I want to".

Learning how to humble ourselves will help us take or accept suggestions and apply those suggestions in our lives. When our sponsors suggest we do something we humble ourselves and trust that he or she has our best interest in mind.

Unfortunately "Humble" is a bad word in the hearts and minds of many inner city people. They define humble as being weak, less than, or punk! Isn't that just like Satan to take one of God's most powerful tools and twist it into something demeaning in the hearts and minds of those that need it. Humbling yourself is not an act of being weak; humbling yourself keeps you teachable and willing. Facing your character defects you being by swallowing your pride.

The Bible says in I Peter 2:1-3, *"Therefore, rid yourselves of all malice and all deceit, hypocrisy, envy, and slander of every kind. (2)Like newborn babies, crave pure spiritual milk, so that by it you may grow up in your salvation, (3 now that you have tasted that the Lord is good."*(NIT) Here Peter is telling us to get rid of all these things that we brought into the kingdom when we accepted the Christ into our lives.

We have to start craving spiritual milk like a newborn babe.   We know that this milk will make us healthy wise and strong. Verse 3 says *"now that you have tasted that the Lord is good"* or, simply put--I didn't get high today, the Lord is good; I'm not out of my mind today, the Lord is good; I'm not sleeping on the street today, the Lord is good, God gave me another chance, the Lord is good. My family is back in my life today, the Lord is good. I have a reason for living today; the Lord is good!

When we humble ourselves it doesn't make us weak it makes us strong! My new definition of humble is "Strength Under Control". It takes a real man/woman to ask for help, to say I'm sorry, to say I don't know. It takes a real man/woman see something in their own life and be willing to change it.

We should come to the Lord with a humble spirit. Remember, God is getting ready to change our lives if we allow Him. There is one thing about God*; He will not make us do anything we do not want to do*. We have to make an effort to change on our own. If we learn to take one step, God will take two for us. Once we start to confront these character defects, we will see that God is right there with us, working things out. We begin by coming to God in the name of Jesus, who is the King of Kings and the Lord of Lords, asking God to take these defects of character from us. *John 16:24 tells us "have ye asked nothing in my name: ask and ye shall receive, that your joy may be full."*

Step 7 goes on to say, "giving us the strength to overcome our faults." We need this strength, because there are things that are deeply embedded in our psyche, or our conscience and sub-conscience mind. Unfortunately, these behaviors make us who we are and they are not fixed overnight, but let this not be an excuse to continue sinning. Once God puts it before you, He will give you everything you need to change that behavior. Some things we do not want to let go of even after we recognize them. This shows us another defect of character--being stubborn and selfish or fearful.

In Step 6, we identify the behaviors that have to be changed. In Step 7, we start working on these behaviors in an honest attempt to rid them from our lives. The bottom line is you can't correct these things in our own power. Here, we humbly petition God with our request to change. Remember recovery is a life changing process, and when there is no change, there is no change!

For instance, how do you change a bad attitude? What do you do about a lying spirit? How do you change your selfish ways? It all begins with humbling yourself before God, because there is no way you can conquer this challenge without God leading and guiding. Only God can make an old man new. We need God to guide, protect, and encourage us to put one foot in front of the other. We are swimming in un-chartered waters, which allow us to go into lands we know nothing about. It would be great if we could be hit by a lighting bolt and change, but it just doesn't work that way.

It takes a willing and a surrendered heart in order for you to be what God wants you to be. It also takes courage to change, an honest effort to recognize the abnormal behavior in action and have a working plan to alter that behavior. A working recovery plan includes:

- Going to meetings and hearing how other people changed as they dealt with the same challenges you are facing now helps to inspire us make the changes needed in our recovery;
- Daily prayer so that God will give you the power to change what he has already revealed to you;
- Educating yourself about your sickness.
- Faith in God. Faith that He will do all that He said He would do. Faith is a verb, which means it is an action word.

We can't sit around and wait for something to happen, we have to take those first steps and God will do the rest. Pray about these faults and God will change your life.

1. Explain humility.

____

____

2. Why is humility important here at this step and in our lives?

____

____

3. What will be your first defect of character that, in your mind, absolutely has to be changed? Why?

____

____

____

4. How has the defect listed in Question #3 hindered your life?

5. How will you attack this character defect next time it raises its ugly head?

6. What is your next character defect you need to change? Why?

Step 8

**Wrote down all those persons we had harmed and became willing to make restitution to them all.
(Matthew 5:23-24, Luke 19:8-10)**

At Step 8, we prepare ourselves by writing down the names of all those people we have harmed in our addiction.

During our days of drinking and using, we hurt so many people and neglected so many responsibilities that it would be impossible to remember them all; but we must make an attempt to reconcile to those God puts before us. Sometimes it is hard to believe that there is any hope of restoring our lives, let alone our relationships with others. We have found that if we are sincere in our prayers, God will work miracles in our lives. Because of our attempt to straighten out our lives by working our program, most people will love and respect us even more. After we start on this road to recovery, and God has forgiven us of all our past sins and wiped our slate clean, it is time to make an effort to mend some of those bridges that we have destroyed. *Matthew 5:23-24 23 So if you are offering your gift at the altar and there remember that your brother has something against you, 24 leave your gift there before the altar and go. First be reconciled to your brother, and then come and offer your gift.* This step is so important to God that he tells us "don't bring nothing to Him until you first fix the rift between your brother".

Here we humble ourselves again and start writing down the names of those people that we have harmed. This is not a time to write down what some of our loved ones did, or are doing to us at the present time. Most of the time they were retaliating or responding in frustration because of something we did in the past. If we really get honest, we will see it was our addictive behavior that caused most of the tension between loved ones and friends.

We must understand that in some cases people will not forgive us because the pain is too severe. But God honors the sincere attempt of reconciliation, which begins with writing the names down on paper. Next we write down what we did to them. Then we pray for the person and about that situation.

Attempting to clean up your past is a very important part of being responsible. No matter how much or how little you did, the time you spent using and abusing drugs or alcohol was time that could have been spent nurturing a relationship. Time you could have used advancing a career, furthering your education, or getting a closer walk with God. Being irresponsible is an area that all addicts and alcoholics have in common. Sometimes the wreckage of our past can seem like a large mountain to climb. But with God, commitment, and treatment, one day at a time all things are possible.

Proverbs 28:13 says, *"He who covers his sins will not prosper, but who ever confesses and forsakes them will have mercy."* In our attempted to grow spiritually and enjoy the blessings of God, we cannot act like we haven't hurt people while we were out using and abusing drugs and alcohol. Being open, honest, and remorseful concerning each situation is the beginning of mercy and it opens the door to the blessings of God.

Even if people do not receive you well, you have done what God wants you to do. God honors the attempt and will bless the effort.

This is not an easy step for some, they hope the loves ones and friends who were injured by their behavior will see that they are in recovery and forgive them. Most recovering people who avoid this step are not truly in recovery.

As we work through Step 8, we take a good look at each love one, friend, and co-worker that we have harmed. From the waitress at the local diner where we made disrespectful drunken passes, to all the people we borrowed money from and never repaid; all should be on the list of reconciliation.

Willingness is the key word in Step 8. We have to be willing to make amends even if the other party is wrong or we think they are wrong. Simply put, God forgave us so we have no reason to carry resentments. Resentment is like a cancer that eats away at all parties involved but for the addict/alcoholic it is a trigger that will lead them back to drinking and using.

Listing those friends and loved ones that we hurt or have been hurt by is only the beginning. There are people who loved us that we are close to and those people relied on us to hold up our end of a relationship. Addicts and alcoholics are notorious for letting our kids down by not being there for them when they were needed the most. Such as appearing at their sports events, their recitals, coming to PTA meetings or just being there for them. Some alcoholics/addicts tend to think that going to work is enough or giving their kids money is enough; but kids need more than that. Supporting them financially is what you're **supposed** to do as a parent. With our family, friends and loved ones, it is our love and companionship that is missed.

For those loved ones and friends with whom we engaged in an altercation, physical or verbal, we have to learn how to forget and forgive even if we don't believe we were the cause. It's not about right or wrong; it's about peace, love, and restoration. It's about learning how to live with your family members and mending the bridges that have been destroyed. This Step is about loving one another. This is the second and greatest commandment.

So many feeling are stirred up when we sit down and begin to attempt this step. "How are they going to treat me?" "What if they turn their backs on me," or "You don't understand what I put them through." You may be right, I don't know what you put them through but God does. One of the greatest statements in the Bible is found in Hebrews 13:5, *"I will never leave you or forsake you" That* is **POWERFUL.** This means *I can do all things through Christ who strengthen me*, (Philippians 4: 13) – even *thought I walk through the valley of the shadows of death I will fear no evil for God the father is with me.* (Psalm 23:4) Begin to write the names of those with whom you will make your amends, and also of those you have harmed. This has to be done because this is right in the site of God.

Once you have written these names, you must pray, fast and meditate, and be willing to ask for forgiveness at the proper time. Share your list with your sponsor. Be ready, because God has a way of putting some of these people in your path a lot sooner than you think.

1. Explain Matthew 6:14-15.

____

____

____

2. Why is this step vital to the addicts' growth?

____

____

3. How does humility play a part in this step?

____

____

4. God said, "I will never leave you or forsake you." What does this mean to you?

____

____

5. Do you really believe your answer?   Yes ☐   No ☐

6. Now that you're here at the eighth Step what is the best way to start this step

____

____

7. List 5 people that you will have to make amends to and why?

1.____

____

2.____

____

3.____

____

4.____

____

5.____

____

8. What part did you play in the "fall" of these relationships? (Use separate paper.) List

only your part.

9. Have you come up with a plan for how you will approach the first three (3) people on
    your list? Yes ☐   No ☐

10. If "no," why haven't you begun? _______________________________________.

11. What is your plan? (Use a blank sheet of paper if necessary)

____

____

____

Step 9

Made direct restitution to such persons whenever possible except when to do so would injure them or others. (James 5:16 Luke 6:31, 36-37)

In Step 8, we prepared ourselves by acknowledging the people we have harmed and forgiven ourselves for the part that we played in the destruction of our relationships.

Here in Step 9 it is time for action. When God puts these people or situations in your path, there are two things you can do. You can avoid this person by quietly going through life as if nothing ever happen, or you can apologize to that person so that you may watch God work a miracle in your life. This Godly act makes you a better person; even if the person does not receive you're apology.

What does the Lord say about restitution? *"The Lord said to Moses: (2) If anyone sins and is unfaithful to the Lord by deceiving his neighbor about something entrusted to him or left in his care or stolen, or if he cheats him, (3)or if he finds lost property and lies about it, or if he swears falsely or, if he commits any such sin that people may do-- (4)when he thus sins and becomes guilty, he must return what he has stolen or taken by extortion, or what was entrusted to him, or the lost property he found, (5)or whatever it was he swore falsely about. He must make restitution in full, add a fifth of the value to it and give it all to the owner of the day he presents his guilt offering."* (Leviticus 6:1- NIV)

Today we seek forgiveness from the people that we have wronged. In some cases, we have to restore, in full, the cost of the property we took. In most cases, our loved ones will be happy to see that we are attempting to straighten out our lives and being honest with them.

When you go in the name of Jesus, there is nothing to be fearful of.   God is with you and He knows you are doing the right thing. Many people find it easy to trust in God when things are going fine and there are no challenges that you must confront. However, to trust in God you must step out on faith not knowing what's going to be the outcome once you make that step. Fear of the unknown will stop many recovering people from taking the next step.   Isaiah 41:10 encourages us by telling us, *"So do not fear, for I am with you; do not be dismayed, for I am your God. I will strengthen you and help you; I will uphold you with my righteous right hand"*

It's time to put your faith into action. It is very easy to say, "I trust God," now it's time to prove it. Do you really believe everything is going to be all right, or do you believe God only answers prayer for other people? , *"Now faith is the substance of thing hoped for; the evidence of things not seen."* (Hebrews 11: 1) Faith is stepping out onto nothing and landing on something; believing everything is going to be all right. If they reject you and your attempts to reconcile with loved ones fail, you have done what God has asked you to do. Today your mission is about doing the right thing. Being responsible, being "right" with yourself and "right" with God. Hope for the best, but you will never know if you don't step out and see. A swimmer never learns to swim standing on the bank. At some point, they have to get into the water.

At Step 9, we also have to use wisdom. The lifestyle that we lived involved a multitude of people and some secrets can't be uncovered because they involve another party. If uncovered this secret would bring pain to you and those involved that have moved on with their lives. Some people and some things you will not be able to address. The severity of the situation might bring harm to everyone involved. Just because you are ready to clean up your life, does not mean everyone is ready to clean up his or her life. For instance, adultery - you cannot tell someone that you had an affair with his or her spouse. This could not only harm you, but the other person who was involved. **USE WISDOM.**

Writing down those you have harmed in the eighth Step is very important. During this time, prayer is also important concerning each injured person. Pray for guidance when facing those you will be making restitution. Humble yourself before family and friends and God will do the rest.

1. How does faith play a part in Step 9?

____

____

2. What do you fear most about sharing with your loved ones or friends?

____

____

____

3. What is the worse thing that can happen if you come clean with your loved ones and friends?

____

____

4. What does the Lord say about restitution?

____

____

Step 10

Examined ourselves daily to see if we are being doers of the Word and not just hearers only. If wrong promptly confess it. (James 1:22, James 5:16, 1 John 1:8-10, Ephesians 4:26)

Step 10 - 11is known as the maintenance step. A lot of information has been received between Steps 1 and 9. On a daily basis, we learn to check in with God to make sure He is pleased with how we lived on that day.

James 1:22 reads, *"But be ye doers of the Word, and not hearers only, deceiving your own selves."* **Examine - To inspect closely, to inquire into carefully, to test by questioning in order to determine progress.**

Take a good look at yourself daily to see if you are following God's Word. We also examine ourselves to make sure we do not allow our behavior that was identified in Step 4 and Step 6 to return. For as recovering addicts/alcoholics it is easy to fall back into our old behavior and our old lifestyle. Five – 10 – 20 years of drinking, using and abusing will easily overpower nine (9) steps of recovery and a few months of clean time.

Honestly examine yourself to see where you are in Christ and where you are in your recovery. Are you going backward, or are you going forward, or are you standing still? *I press toward the mark for the prize of the high calling of God in Christ Jesus.* (Philippians 3:14) God forbid anyone finds themselves going backwards in their walk with the Lord. Going backwards or standing still in your walk with God is cause for an addict/alcoholic to surely relapse. One of God's goals for every Christian is to go higher in Him.

Those that stand still get caught by the enemy, which is always looking for someone that has gotten complacent in their walk with God. The Bible says in I Peter 5:8, *"Be sober, be vigilant; because your adversary the devil, as a roaring lion, walketh about, seeking whom he may devour."* Those that stand still get caught. Those that stand still start believing that they are normal and can do some of the things that they used to do before recovery. They begin associating with people that are detrimental to their new way of life. These people cosign their old lifestyle and slowly the enemy fools them. They slowly begin to pick up some of those bad habits that were the cause of their drinking and using, always justifying their actions with another excuse.

We must examine ourselves daily to see if we were living the way God would have us to live. It says in *John 8:32, you shall know the truth and the truth shall make you free.* The word *"know"* in the Greek translation means to *live, or recognize truth by personal experience.* Living God's truth everyday is our goal. We know we cannot be perfect people, but in Christ, we keep striving to be the best Christians that we can be.

Ephesians 4:26 [26] *"In your anger do not sin" Do not let the sun go down while you are still angry.* The Word of God continues to make us better. This application if applied will make anyone a better person. It helps you to take a good look at yourself, and if willing you strive to be a better person. There would not be as much pain in the body nor in the world today, if there were more doers of the Word striving to be their best in Christ.

In our everyday life, it is so easy to be led astray and caught up in worldly or fleshly ways. The Bible says in Matthew 7:23, *"Enter through the narrow gate. For wide is the gate and broad is the road that leads to destruction, and many enter through it. But small is the gate and narrow the road that leads to life, and only a few find it. Those who seek the Lord will find the way."* Many people are on the wrong road in life and they don't know it because they don't examine themselves to see where they are.

During our meditation or quiet time, before we get on our knees to ask God to forgive us our sins, we should think about our day. Think about how we handled various situations, where we fell short, or held our peace. We need to ask for forgiveness and get a better understanding of how we could have handled these situations. Motives play a big part in why we do some of the things we do. If our motives are self-serving, or financially motivated, it alters the way we handle different situations. Our goal is to become better Christians, and it will take searching our *own* self and honestly examining our actions and re-actions and doing our best to live a better life.

One of the most powerful components of this disease of addiction is its uncanny way of causing the recovering addict/alcoholic to forget just how bad it used to be before recovery. Knowing that drinking and using brings nothing but pain and destruction, a recovering addict/alcoholic will pick up a drink or a hit and return to that old lifestyle. Did they forget about the jails, institutions, and the walking death? Did they forget the lost of jobs, the separation from family and friends? Surely, they forgot that the disease of addiction centers in our mind; as long as a person can remember it is a possibility that they can return to drinking and using. When they stop going to meetings and stop working their program they tend to believe they are well; and, thus, they are on their way to relapse.

An addict/alcoholic enters into relapse mode when they think they have arrived! They believe they are normal and can go back to drinking and using like normal people. Deep down they don't believe in the disease concept. Because of the program they feel good about themselves and they've been deceived by Satan. This step reminds you to never arrive and to continue working on yourself.

Here at the 10th Step, we daily examine ourselves to make sure we continue doing everything we did to get free in-order to stay free. Are we still praying, are we still making meetings, are we still spending time with our sponsors? Are we still pressing toward the mark that God has set for us? What kind of Christian are you today, are you still on fire for the Lord like the day you came into the program, or when you first entered into the presence of God? Or have you become just a Sunday Christian who only shows up to Church on Sundays with half-hearted worship, half-hearted prayer and half-hearted thanksgiving? Or do you even go to Church anymore? Are you still able to take constructive criticism, without getting angry? Are you still willing to change?

Things to look at while examining yourself daily are:
1) Has unnecessary "drama" returned to your life?
2) Have you begun to separate yourself from family and friends?
3) Are you hanging out with old friends, or new friends that do not keep God first?
4) Has your relationship with God gotten better, worse, or about the same since you began this road to recovery?

It is easy to fall if we don't continue to keep God first and your recovery second. Anything else will be detrimental to your well-being.

1. What is the difference between being a "hearer" of the Word and a "doer" of the Word?

____

____

2. Why "examine ourselves" daily?

____

____

3. What part of the day will you be "examining yourself" and why?

____

____

4. What happens to a person that stands still in the Lord?

____

____

5. John 8:32 says, *"You shall know the truth and the truth shall make you free."* What is the Greek translation for the word "know"? Why is it important to this step?

____

____

6. Recovery is a process and our goal is to continue to grow. Have you stopped growing?

    Yes ☐   No ☐

7. If "No", what are you doing to continue growing in the Lord? If "Yes", what is the problem? What will it take to get back on track and continue growing?

____

____

8. Has unnecessary "drama" returned to your life?   Yes ☐   No   ☐

9. Have you begun to separate yourself from family and friends? Yes ☐   No ☐

10. Are you hanging out with old friends, or new friends that do not keep God first?
     Yes ☐ No   ☐

11.   Has your relationship with God gotten better, worse, or about the same since you
began this road to recovery?

____

____

12. Do you still pray as much as you did when you were seeking help from God on the first
     Step?   Yes ☐   No   ☐

13. Do you still praise God as much?   Yes ☐ No   ☐

14. Do you still read Gods Word as much? Yes ☐ No   ☐

Step 11

Continue to pray, study and meditate on the Word, and maintain consistent fellowship with believers to improve our relationship with God. (Joshua 1:8, Psalms 1:1-3, 1 Thessalonians 5:17, 2 Timothy 2:15, Hebrews 10:25)

Most addicts/alcoholics relapse when they stop doing the things that got them clean or sober in the first place. An addict will get 6 months, 9 months, 1 year, 2 years, 3 years, of clean and sober time and for whatever reason, some will stop praying, stop studying the Word, stop fellowshipping (going to 12 Step meetings). Soon they find themselves drawn back into their old lifestyle practicing their disease even more often than before.

The Bible says in *Matthew 12:43-45, "When an unclean spirit goes out of a man, he goes through dry places, seeking rest, and finds none, (44) Then he says, "I will return to my house from which I came." And when he comes, he finds it empty, swept, and put in order. (45)"Then he goes and takes with him seven other spirits more wicked than himself, and they enter and dwell there; and the last state of that man is worse than the first. So shall it also be with this wicked generation."* It is plain to see that the wicked spirit leaves the alcoholic/addict and roams around seeking a place to rest. Then it returns to find the house is empty, swept, and put in order. There is nothing there to fight off old temptations. No tools to recognize triggers that lead to drinking and using. We, in recovery call this a dry drunk. This house is so empty even the spirit of the Lord has been put out. So the evil spirit returns with seven of its evil friends and makes life even worse than before for the recovering person.

For the addict/alcoholic who is involved in the process of recovery, relapse is always a risk. It is Satan's job to deceive you into thinking you do not need to continue making your meetings, studying the Word, and fellowshipping with the saints. When you stop, you actually stop taking the medicine for your disease. If you don't take your medicine, you will get sick. Satan's job is to steal, kill, and destroy your life; if you give him an inch, he will take a mile.

Your direct line to the Father, through Jesus, is prayer. God is waiting to hear from you. God is our Father and we are His children. God wants to develop a personal relationship with you. We who have been rescued from Satan's plan to kill us should not be naive to the fact that Satan wants us back. We have to always be on guard with our armor on. Luke 22:40 says, *"Pray that you will not fall into temptation."* Matthew 26:41 tells us to, *"Watch and pray so that you will not fall into temptation."* In both cases, the Word of God tells us it is easy to fall, drop, descend, and plunge into temptation. In all my years of working with addicts and alcoholics that relapse, I have discovered that the cause is never clear.

We have to study to understand God's character, to understand how we should live; embracing righteousness and living holy. Perfecting love, grace, humility, peace, joy, happiness, and what is right will be the goals we strive for. By studying God's Word, we grow in the knowledge of Him. The Bible says in II Timothy 2:15, *"Study to show thyself approved unto God, a workman that needeth not to be ashamed, rightly dividing the word of truth."*

Did you know that there is a difference between reading and studying? There is also a difference between studying and living. John 8:32 says *you shall know the truth and the truth shall make you free.* The Greek translation for "know" is *live.* So *you shall live the truth and the truth shall make you free.* Most Christians that struggle with drugs and alcohol understand studying the Word of God, but they have a hard time living what they've study. The Bible says in Hosea 4:6, *"My people are destroyed from a lack of knowledge."* Living what we know will be the key to our growth and to building a solid foundation in Christ Jesus.

Fellowshipping with believers will strengthen the walk of the recovering person. Hebrews 10:25 says, *"Let us not give up meeting together, as some are in the habit of doing, but let us encourage one another---and all the more as you see the day approaching."* Here we see where fellowship is important. The 11th Step reminds us to continue fellowshipping with people just like ourselves--recovering addicts/alcoholics. Meeting people in Christ-centered 12 Step fellowship meetings (Free N One) is an important part of our recovery.   Getting involved in Church activities and Church auxiliaries is also an excellent place to meet new Christian friends.   We   suggest three meetings a week, one Bible study, and Church on Sunday. Some may think it's a lot because the addict/alcoholic is always looking for a quick fix. It's going to take everything you've got to restore you back to sanity and to develop a right relationship with God.

The 10th and 11th Steps are referred to as Maintenance Steps in the recovery process. Here we focus on building a solid foundation in God, preparing for the storms that lie ahead for the recovering person.

God will begin to take you down new avenues that you have never faced before. Many addicts and alcoholics get to this point and they turn back to drinking and using because of fear. Fear of success, fear of change, and fear of the unknown; these things cause us to turn and run. We have to trust that God has our best interest at heart. We have to believe that he knows what He is doing. Our prayers and constant contact with God will strengthen our faith in God, enabling us to walk boldly through any situation.

Pray without ceasing, study to know God for yourself. Meditation also plays a vital part in recovery. Meditation can be hours of quiet time concentrating on God and His Glory, or it can be just taking five (5) minutes out of your day to be still and acknowledge that He is God.

We also have to be aware that Satan is upset with us because we have turned and walked away from him. He knows what we were drawn to in the world. Worldly things that were revealed to us in our fourth Step and our sixth Step will all be readily - used by Satan to get us back. Be prepared for an all out attack on the flesh, and it will come, so you must be deeply rooted in God to withstand the attack.

Pray, meditate and study God's Word one day at a time as we enter into the days of our reconstruction. Sometimes there will be days when different and exciting things will be happening to the recovering addict/alcoholic. Then there will be days when nothing is going on and you wonder if God still there. It is days like these when it is easy to fall into being content, we slowly get used to it, and we enter into a dangerous area. The Bible says in Proverbs 19:15, *"Laziness cast one into deep sleep, and an idle person will suffer hunger."* If we don't continue to do the things that freed us from that bondage we will "fall asleep" and find ourselves on the wrong road, headed back to a lifestyle of destruction.

MAKE YOUR MEETINGS, FELLOWSHIP WITH BELIEVERS, AND STICK WITH THE WINNERS

1. What happens when an evil spirit leaves a dwelling goes away for a while, then returns and finds it empty?

____

____

2. What is your prayer life like? Very good ☐   Good ☐   Okay ☐   Bad ☐

3. Are you satisfied with your answer?   Yes ☐   No ☐

4. What can you do to make it better?

____

____

5. What is your study life like? Very good ☐   Good ☐   Okay ☐   Bad ☐

6. Are you satisfied with your answer?   Yes ☐   No ☐

7. What can you do to make it better?

____

____

8. Do you spend quiet time with the Lord? (Meditation) Yes ☐ No ☐ When you first started making meetings, you attended # ____ meetings a week. How many meetings are you making now? #_____

9. Are you happy with your answer?   Yes ☐   No ☐

    If "Yes" why? If "No" why?

____

____

"I freed a thousand slaves
and could have freed a
thousand more if they only
knew they were slaves"

Harriet Tubman

Step 12

Having had a born again experience and having been freed from our addiction, we shared our testimony with those who are still in bondage and continued to be doers of the Word in all our affairs.   (Matthew 28:19-20, Romans 1:16, Galatians 5:1 and 13, 1 Timothy 6:18, John 3:3)

As we approach Step 12, many changes have taken place in the recovering person's life. Because of this modern day miracle, the recovering addict/alcoholic has to ask one very important question: Why? Why did God choose me to be free from this addiction that is destroying thousands everyday? Once you start enjoying this new life, you honor God by finding out why God choose you. Now that you are enjoying this freedom, understand that you are in no way out of the woods; but now you can be certain you are on the right road. It is time you look back to where God brought you from by asking questions such as why? Why was God watching over you while you were using and abusing drugs and alcohol? Why did God protect you while you were locked up in jail, or caught in a dope deal that went bad? How did your car make it home while you were drunk and out of your mind? Why you are still here? If you have not asked yourself these questions, maybe you should return to Step 1 and begin this process all over again.

Some of us were not only delivered from certain destruction due to the lifestyle we lived. There are some of us who worked for Satan himself. We sold dope, we turned people on to dope, used and abused people along the way; and God turned around and save our lives.   You have to ask yourself, "Why me, God?"

Now that you have arrived at this 12th Step and God has only begun to restore order back into your life, it is time to give back what so freely was given to you. Who can better share with someone that wants to be free from drugs and alcohol than you?   God saved you for a reason, and that reason is to tell someone who is still bound by this disease how they can be free.

Sometimes I wonder how God looks at a person that He has set free from drug or alcohol addiction, and this person gets involved in the Church, but never tells anyone what God has done for him. Why? Is it you that don't want anyone to know that you were a dope-fiend, a junkie, or maybe a drunk, an alcoholic? The most important word in this statement is "were". You used to be and alcoholic or junkie. If you find it uncomfortable to share what God has delivered you from because of what people might think, then you have to go back to the Step 6 and ask God to help you with "fear" and "people pleasing." The Bible says at 2 Timothy 1:8-9, *"So do not be ashamed to testify about our Lord, or ashamed of me his prisoner. But join with me in suffering for the gospel, by the power of God, ⁹who has saved us and called us to a holy life--not because of anything we have done but because of his own purpose and grace. This grace was given us in Christ Jesus before the beginning of time."*

It is our testimony that will get the attention of those that are still suffering. It is our testimony that will give hope to those that want to be free. I, personally, have a problem with people who become "secret agent Christians." God delivers them from drug or alcohol addiction and they are embarrassed about the life they used to lead. "Secret agent Christians" that sit in Church with this covered-up miracle and they keep it secret because of their position in the Church; they sweep that part of their life under a rug, never to let it out again. The Bible also says at Mark 8:38, *"If anyone is ashamed of me and my words in this adulterous and sinful generation, the Son of Man will be ashamed of him when he comes in his Father's glory with the holy angels."*

God purposely send people to us so that we can share our testimony with them; but, because of what others might think, we never share that part of our life. Where were these people when you were bound in your addiction "tow-up from the flow-up?" Where were these people when your family turned their backs on you and now God is restoring even that? We pray that you will not forget the pain you once were in. How can you act like you never went through this period in your life when God allowed it to happen for a reason? Hidden miracles are all over this nation, waiting for God to get the glory. I am sure if God were still adding pages to the Bible, some of our stories would be in there-- modern day miracles.

We have a saying in this process called recovery, "I was saved to serve," bottom line. You cannot be blessed with this freedom and keep it to yourselves. Too many of God's people are dying because no one has met them where they are with their testimony. We beg of you, never forget where you came from. Somebody needs to hear your story. Tell somebody in bondage just what God has done for you. After you have shared with them, be a committee of one and take them to a Free N One meeting. (Each one teach one.) Once God has taken you from the pit of hell, picked you up, and cleaned you up, God expects you to share with others, especially those who are suffering from drug and alcohol addiction.

For some reason, there are people think that what God has done for them, (delivered them from drugs and alcohol) He was supposed to do. No! It was God's GRACE and MERCY that spared you.

What we have received from God is a modern day miracle. This miracle is just as big as God parting the Red Sea, or Jesus walking on water. It's equally as significant as Jesus raising Lazarus from the dead. Matter of fact we were dead, we just hadn't laid down yet. We cannot take for granted what God has done for us. We should be excited about this modern day miracle, giving God the glory for what He has done in our lives.

Some people ponder over what ministry they should pursue, or pray about what field they should be involved in, and rightfully so. Maybe you want to sing in the choir, join the usher board, or even work in children's Church. Maybe God has called you to be a deacon or minister, or pastor of your own Church. However, whatever it is, you can rest assured that a person afflicted by this disease of addiction will cross your path. It will be your job to show love by taking them by the hand, walking with them until they can walk on their own. Some people believe it's the Pastor's job, or even the Church's job. No, it's your job. If your Church starts a Christ-centered support group, you should be there for support. How will people know God works if they don't see what God has done for you? If your Church does not have a drug program, go to your Pastor and request to start one.

To keep what God has done for you a secret would be a sin. Addicts and alcoholics that have been rescued by the power of God should yell it from the mountaintop and let everyone know that it was God and only God who saved their lives.

One way to do this is to attend many meetings. Not only will you be helping yourself, but also you will be helping others who still do not believe that they can be free or are struggling with this process.   There are many newcomers attending meetings and they need to hear and see other delivered addict/alcoholics there sharing about their experiences, strength and hope.

Matthew 9:37-38 says, *"Then Jesus sayeth unto his disciples, The harvest truly is plenteous, but the laborers are few; (38)Pray ye therefore the Lord of the harvest, that he will send forth laborers into his harvest. You are part of that harvest."* This scripture lets us know that there are many people out there suffering, just waiting to hear the good news of Jesus Christ.

It is fitting that this last Step lines up with God's greatest commission that is found at Matthew 28:18-20, *"All authority has been given to Me in heaven and on earth. (19)Go therefore and make disciples of all the nations, baptizing them in the name of the Father and of the Son and of the Holy Spirit, (20)teaching them to observe all things that I have commanded you; and lo, I am with you always, even to the end of the age."*

Verse 20 says, "*Observe all things that I have commanded you*," meaning don't stray away from the Word of God. We should live righteous and holy, and God will be with you always.

Continue to grow in the Lord. One of the biggest problems with being free from drugs and alcohol is that we tend to get "well" and we forget where we came from and what kind of person we used to be. The disease of addiction centers in your mind, and as long as you can remember the disease of addiction is with you.

Humble yourself at all times; the thorn in your flesh is still there. As you humble yourself, God will give you strength to share everywhere you go. Stay willing. Stay open. Not only will you be a blessing to someone else, but God will bless you also. This is a motto that we as recovering people should live by:

I WAS SAVED TO SERVE

1. Out of all the people in the world, why do you think God saved you?

____

____

2. Why must the recovering addict/alcoholic not forget where they have come from?

____

____

____

3. What has God called you to do?

____

____

4. What does "I was saved to serve" mean?

____

____

5. Who first told you about God? _________________________

6. Who told you about this program? _______________________

7. Where would you be if no one ever gave you this great information?

____

8. If you were to save someone's life and they never said thank you, how do you think you would feel?

____

9. Are you involved in any ministries in your Church? Yes ☐ No ☐

10. If yes, what ministry? If no, why not?

____

____

11. By the time you get to Step 12, you should be helping someone. Who is that person? (I hope your answer is not blank)

____

____

Chapter *IV*

SUMMARY

What Did You Learn From This Process Called Recovery?
How Can It Help You?

For the Addict/Alcoholic:

1. The process of recovery is an on-going, never ending process.
2. You cannot get this thing called "recovery" overnight.
3. You must have a sponsor to walk you through this process.
4. You must make meetings, and participate in these meeting by getting honest and sharing.
5. Live the Word and you will be free.
6. You must change because when there is no change, there is no change.
7. It takes work to change.
5. Remember this disease of addiction is a sickness.
6. You must work/live the Steps.
7. You must continue to pray.

For the family member:

1. Allow the recovering person to make as many meetings as possible.
2. When they are not making meetings, they are in relapse mode.
3. Do not, I repeat, do not work their program with them. Don't go to their meetings with them; don't volunteer to be their sponsors.
4. Don't be afraid to ask, "What Step are they on?"
5. Get to know their sponsor. Ask the sponsor to be honest with you and call you if the person stops making their meetings.
6. This process of recovery takes time, so be patient.
7. Remember this disease of addiction is a sickness.
8. You should attend Free N One Tough Love meetings.
9. Remember, God is in control, not you!
10. Continue to pray.

Church Auxiliary Leader:

If you know of a person who comes out of a recovery home:

1. Be careful when allowing a recovering person to be a part of your auxiliary or ministry. Many will take on more than they can handle, or they think being involved with different ministries will fix them. They must continue their meetings.
2. We suggest the recovering person wait at least 6 months before joining a ministry. One year before leading a ministry or auxiliary.

Employers:

If the recovering person comes back from a leave of absent because of their addiction, or you find that he/she has a problem, please consider the following:

1. Recovery Card. This card will list the meetings this person is attending (see example on last page).
2. This is between you and the recovering person. No one else should know unless he/she decides to tell someone.
1. Remember the alcoholism/addiction is a disease
2. Keep all information confidential.
3. Do not include this information in their personnel file, but keep it in the medical records file.

Go to our webpage and see

the work we are doing. Join

us, support us, and most of

all continue to pray for us!

www.free-n-one.org

FREE N ONE

The drug and alcohol free program Free N One – (Free from drugs and alcohol, and one in Christ.)

THE PURPOSE OF FREE N ONE IS:

1. To establish, provide, and maintain inter-city drug and alcohol free meetings centered in the Church.
2. To teach the addict/alcoholic how to be free through the 12 Spiritual Steps to Recovery and the Process of Recovery.
3. To establish a safe place for people who are addicted to drugs or alcohol and want to be free. (A safe place is a Church that will not judge them because of their illness.)
4. To educate the Church about the disease of addiction.
5. To provide help for the family and significant others through drug/alcohol support group meetings called Tough Love.
6. To assist the recovered addict and re-establish him/her in the community by providing funds for continuing education or network for job placement and referrals.
7. To bring the Church together as one; to fight this affliction that is destroying our people, our cities, and our nation.
8. To educate the family member about codependency and how to be free from the perils of the practicing addict/alcoholic. (Remember God gave you a life, are you living it or are you taking care of the addict/alcoholic?)

In 1987, the founder of Free N One, Ronald Simmons, now Reverend Ronald Wright, and Minister Rene Whitehead came together in response to a need. This need was an outpatient drug and alcohol program designed for the Church, rooted in the Word of God, led by the Spirit of God. After weeks of meetings and months of planning, the founders established Free N One, the drug and alcohol free program. All three men are recovering alcoholics/addicts. Having given their lives over to God, and while in recovery, they noticed that something was missing in the care of the addict/alcoholic and something had to be done. They recognized that the most powerful organization in the community (the Church) was silent concerning the disease of addiction. They also knew that the only answer to the drug and alcohol problem is the power of God through the Church. One Church standing alone cannot win this war. It is going to take the whole body to defeat this demon called addiction.

Free N One brings each Church together with the same agenda, the same goals and objectives, all serving the same God. There is no one Church bigger or better than another. We all stand together in unity with one common goal, "Freedom" through Jesus Christ our Lord and Savior. There are many reasons why we believe the Church should adopt Free N One. The most important reasons are that it is spiritually and clinically sound, **and that it works**.